MANAGIN

About the authors

Margaret Allen is a marketing communications consultant who has worked in leading agencies such as Saatchi & Saatchi and McCann Erickson. She now runs Marketing Advantage (UK), a communication and training consultancy. She is a course director and faculty member of the Chartered Institute of Marketing and works extensively with Henley Management College.

Judith Bridge spent her first ten years in marketing working for Unilever on their detergent and personal care products. She now occupies a senior marketing role at United Biscuits.

Paul Eastwood began in advertising as an Art Director the day man landed on the moon. His 'giant step' was a trade ad for BT. Consumer campaigns followed and he soon won an award for Pentax. His BP work gained him entrance to the prestigious Design and Art Directors' Association. He became Head of Art, Group Head, Deputy Creative Director, Creative Director and European Creative Director all in the right order, all at different agencies. Along the way he became responsbile for major brands like Zanussi, BT, LWT, C&A, Domestos and Surf. Now, as an independent, he runs his own marketing consultancy, writes scripts and produces corporate films for his own production company and is one of the Chartered Institute of Marketing's regular speakers on creativity. Despite all this he is happily married with two children and an unruly jazz collection.

Gavin M Galloway was born in Middlesex, England of Scots descent and educated at Oxford and LSE. He has worked variously in market research, makreting and new product development over the years. He is an occasional supporter of Watford FC and a resolute real ale drinker.

Rosemary Gorman has worked in the advertising industry for the past 18+ years. Her time has been spent planning and buying media in various agencies including Geers Gross, McCann Erickson and Zenith Media. Rosemary is currently Head of Media Planning and Managing Partner at Zenith Media, the UK's number one Media Independent. Her experience covers all sectors from financial to retail and across all media. She is also a member of the IPA and Marketing Society.

Managing Advertising

Editor
Margaret Allen

BLACKHALL
Publishing

This book was typeset by KRISTIN JENSEN for

BLACKHALL PUBLISHING
26 Eustace Street
Dublin 2
Ireland

e-mail: blackhall@tinet.ie

© Margaret Allen, 1999

ISBN: 1 901657 51 5

A catalogue record for this book is available from the British Library.

All rights reserved. No part of this publication may be reproduced, stored in a retrieval system or transmitted in any form or by any means, electronic, mechanical, photocopying, recording or otherwise, without the prior, written permission of the publisher.

This book is sold subject to the condition that it shall not, by way of trade or otherwise, be lent, resold, hired out, or otherwise circulated without the publisher's prior consent in any form of binding or cover other than that in which it is published and without a similar condition including this condition being imposed on the subsequent purchaser.

Printed in Ireland by
Wood Printcraft

Contents

INTRODUCTION .... *xv*

PART 1: THE DEVELOPMENT OF ADVERTISING

ONE: UNDERSTANDING ADVERTISING POTENTIAL 1
1.1: *The Versatility of Advertising* 1
1.2: *Potential Advertising Objectives* 2
      Create Sales 2
      Create Awareness 3
      Alter Perceptions and Attitudes 3
      Create Desires 4
      Provide Reassurance 5
      Remind 5
      Give Reasons for Buying 5
      Consolidate a Position to Protect
        against the Competition 6
      Demonstrate 6
      Generate Enquiries 6
      Increase Traffic 6
      What do we Want Advertising to Communicate? 7
1.3: *Understanding Benefits and Insights* 8
      Benefits 8
      Benefit Analysis 9
      What Makes Up a Benefit? 9
1.4: *Rational versus Emotional Benefits* 10
      Rational Benefits 10
      Emotional Benefits 11
      What is Insight? 12

TWO: STARTING THE ADVERTISING DEVELOPMENT PROCESS 15
      How Does Advertising Fit
        into the Marketing Concept? 15
2.1: *The Marketing Concept* 17
      Portfolio Positioning 17

Competitive Strategy 18
Target Consumer Segment 18
Competitive Advantage 18
Focused Marketing Mix 18
2.2: Conduct a Strategic Trawl 19
What? 20
Who is our Target Consumer? 21
Why do we Need to Communicate with Them? 21
Where should our Communication be Seen? 22
When should our Communication be Seen? 22
How should we be Communicating
 with our Target? 22
How Much? 23
2.3: Choosing Between Communication Tools 23
Advertising 24
Direct Marketing 25
Sales Promotion 26
Public Relations 27
Sponsorship 28
Exhibitions 28
Merchandising 29
2.4: Integrated Communication 30

THREE: RESEARCH FOR ADVERTISING DEVELOPMENT 33
3.1: Research and Information for Brand
 Marketing Planning 33
The Brand Review Process 34
Key Elements of the Brand Review Process 35
Key Research Processes 36
3.2: Using the Brand Review Process to Set Brand
 Marketing Objectives and Strategy 37
Setting Communication Objectives 37
3.3: Research and Information Prior to the
 Creative Brief 38
3.4: Research to Reappraise the Brand Positioning 40
Benefit Generation 40
3.5: Research for Creative Development 41
Objectives of Research 41

3.6: How is the Advertising Idea Presented
    to the Consumer? 43
        Television/Cinema Advertising 44
        Press/Poster Advertising 44
3.7: Pre-testing 45
        Assessment of Effect in the Marketplace 45
        Pre-testing Sales Effect 45
        Pre-testing Brand Effect 46
        Which Measures are Important for our Brand? 47
        How do we Interpret the Scores? 48
        Assessment of how the Advertising is
            Working (or Not) 49
        Guidelines for Using Pre-tests 49

FOUR: THE ADVERTISING PRODUCTION PROCESS 51
4.1: Creative Services 51
        Traffic Control 51
        Art Buyers 51
        Photographers/Illustrators 52
4.2: Client Presentation to Finished Execution 52
        Pre-Pre-Production Meeting 54
        Pre-Production Meeting 55
        Advertising Agency Producer 56
        Producers and Directors 56
        Pre-Production and Final Pre-production Meeting 58
        Filming 59
        Post-Production Stage 61

FIVE: ASSESSING THE EFFECTS OF ADVERTISING 63
5.1: Sustaining/Developing Brands 63
5.2: Influencing Consumer Behaviour 64
5.3: Brands 64
        Brand Model 65
        Implications for Advertising 65
        Communicating the Brand Positioning 66
        Basic Role/Objectives of Advertising 66
        Brand Situation 67
5.4: Setting Specific Advertising Objectives 68

5.5: The Evaluation of Advertising Effects 69
5.6: Evaluation of Advertising Effects on
 Consumer Behaviour 69
    Direct Evaluation of Consumer Behaviour 72
    Indirect Evaluation of Consumer Behaviour 73
    Evaluating Advertising Effects vs Other Effects
    on Consumer Behaviour 73
5.7: Evaluation of Brand Effects on Advertising 76
5.8: Direct Effects on the Brand 76
    Brand Salience 76
    Consumer Perceptions of the Brand 77
    Consumer Feelings Towards the Brand 79
5.9: Evaluating the Direct Effects of Advertising
 on the Brand: Short-Term vs Long-Term 82
5.10: Consumer/Advertising Interaction 82

PART 2: ADVERTISING AGENCIES

SIX: ADVERTISING AGENCY STRUCTURE AND FUNCTION 87
6.1: Account Management 88
6.2: Planning 89
6.3: Creative 89
    Copywriter 90
    Art Director 90
6.4: Production 90
    Press and Print Production 91
    Television and Radio Production 91
6.5: Media 92
    Planning and Non-Television Buying 92
    Television Buyer 93
    Media Research/Intelligence 94
6.6: Finance 94
6.7: Appointing an Advertising Agency 94
    Assessing Competing Agencies 96
6.8: The Competitive Pitch 97
6.9: Appraisal of Advertising Agencies 100
6.10: Agency Remuneration 102

  Decline in Rates of Commission 103
  Fee System 104
  Payment by Results 104

SEVEN: DEVELOPING AN AGENCY BRIEF
 AND THE BRIEFING PROCESS **107**
7.1: Brand Essence 108
  Outer Layers 109
  Inner Layers 110
  Core 110
7.2: Brand Positioning Statement 110
  The Brand Positioning Statement Headings 111
  The Market 112
  Consumer Target 112
  Further Supporting Analysis 112
  Brand Positioning Summary Statement 113
7.3: Communication Mix Statement 113
7.4: Creative Brief 114
7.5: Towards the Perfect Brief 117
7.6: The Briefing Meeting 119
7.7: The Internal Agency Creative Brief 122

EIGHT: MAKING THE CLIENT/AGENCY RELATIONSHIP WORK **124**
8.1: The Agency Perspective: What Contributes to a
 Good Client Relationship? 124
  Timing 124
  Briefing 125
  Creative Judgement 126
  Administration 127
  Teamwork 128
8.2: The Client Perspective: What Contributes to a
 Good Agency Relationship? 129
  Understanding the Client's Business 129
  Strategic Thinking 130
  Creative Process 131
  Administration 132

PART 3: PRACTICAL APPLICATIONS

NINE: UNDERSTANDING CREATIVE WORK 137
9.1: Defining an Idea 138
9.2: The Creative Process 140
9.3: Judging Creative Work 142
9.4: Involving the Consumer 144

TEN: UNDERSTANDING THE MEDIA MARKETPLACE 147
10.1: National Press 148
10.2: Magazines 149
      Magazine Sectors 150
      Reader Relationship 150
10.3: Cinema 151
      Advantages 152
      Disadvantages 152
      Cinema Airtime 152
10.4: Outdoor Advertising 153
      Advantages 153
      Outdoor Market Structure 154
10.5: Television 155
      ITV 156
      Channel 4 157
      Channel 5 158
      Satellite/Cable 158
10.6: Radio 159

ELEVEN: MEDIA PLANNING PRINCIPLES 162
11.1: Advertising Planning 162
11.2: Developing the Media Strategy 163
      Who is the Target Consumer? 163
      Media Research 164
      Demographic Data 164
      Target Group Index (TGI) 164
11.3: Selecting the Medium 165
11.4: What Prompts a Response? 167
      Television Rating Point 168
11.5: Coverage 169

11.6: Frequency 170
11.7: Where do I Advertise? 172
11.8: What Does an Advertising Campaign Cost? 173
11.9: Do I Have the Right Plan? 174

GLOSSARY **177**

LIST OF HELPFUL ADDRESSES **212**

INDEX **215**

Thanks to Gav, Paul, Rosemary and Jude for putting up with my endless nagging to get this book off the ground.

I told you we could do it!

Introduction

When compiling this book I had in the back of my mind many clients and agency staff with whom I have worked in my role as an agency account director and latterly as a communications and training consultant. In my experience there continues to be gaps in both client and agency understanding on ways of optimising the advertising development process. These gaps can sometimes be difficult to fill, as the advertising development process is essentially multi-skilled and multi-disciplinary.

Advertising management covers everything from strategic marketing thinking at one end of the spectrum to appraisal of production quotes at the other. I believe that there are very few individuals who would be comfortable conversing knowledgeably on the entire advertising process. For this reason I believed that it was not possible for one person to write a book on the management of advertising, hence I have called on a range of specialists from account management, the creative and planning departments within adverting agencies and from a client marketing department. This 'combining of knowledge' has inevitably resulted in slight variations in writing style between some of the chapters.

For a discipline that is essentially learnt 'on the job' we have attempted to pull together the essentials of this management process, which will be useful to both agencies and clients alike. Hopefully, for both parties this is an indispensable guide in helping to understand and manage the entire process to achieve the goal of not just effective but outstanding advertising.

Part 1

THE DEVELOPMENT OF ADVERTISING

Chapter 1
Understanding Advertising Potential

It is likely that for many companies, advertising presents itself as playing a leading role in the communication plan. Why does advertising continue to form the backbone of communication plans when there are so many other less costly communication tools available? Quite simply, it is because advertising is versatile, extremely visible and continues to have one of the best track records in fulfilling pre-determined communication objectives.

There is undoubtedly a wealth of great advertising that is talked about, and it can even become part of popular culture. There is also a vast amount of mediocre advertising that fails to break through the clutter of communication messages that we are constantly bombarded with. How can it be ensured that advertising messages are optimised and achieve their desired effect?

1.1 THE VERSATALITY OF ADVERTISTING

The first hurdle to be overcome is to recognise that versatility, one of the undoubted strengths of advertising, is also one of its major potential weaknesses. Advertising is capable of fulfilling so many communication objectives that it is tempting to write a shopping list of the things we wish our advertising to achieve. Imagine that a new food product is to be launched. A marketing department could easily write objectives for the advertising as follows:

> *To increase awareness and change perceptions of our product by communicating its high quality and superior taste delivery over the competition whilst also incentivising trade and consumer alike to stock and purchase.*

At first sight, these may seem like entirely reasonable objectives for a campaign to fulfil, but on closer examination check how many objectives this campaign has been set.

1. Increase awareness.
2. Change perceptions.
3. Communicate product information.
4. Make a competitive superiority statement.
5. Incentivise trade listing.
6. Incentivise consumer purchase.

One single communication task has set six objectives! It may be possible to accomplish this, but experience has shown that the less single-minded the communication objectives, the more confusing the resultant communication is likely to be. Such a communication would be unlikely to achieve any of these objectives well, let alone six! How do we ensure that the shopping list approach is avoided? The first step is to be aware of the range and scope of objectives that advertising can fulfil.

1.2 POTENTIAL ADVERTISING OBJECTIVES

This list is in no way intended to be exhaustive, but it serves to highlight the fact that choices have to be made early in the planning process about the role advertising is to fulfil.

Create Sales

For many companies this is the ultimate objective. Without sales they would cease to exist. It is an obvious, if not the most obvious, reason to advertise. There should be no need to feel embarrassed about being clear on the brand ambitions in the marketplace. The sales targets should be made clear but should also be realistic. It is becoming common practice for advertising agencies to receive 'payment by results'. This may be in the form of an additional bonus if sales objectives are reached. It should be recognised that advertising alone cannot achieve sales miracles – if the product is not listed by major outlets, ambitious sales targets are extremely unlikely to be achieved.

For many companies, this is the easiest and most straightforward objective to set. It is also useful to set additional/secondary objectives that will add to the longer-term brand health, e.g. brand goodwill scores.

Create Awareness

This is another fundamental advertising objective which is frequently set. It can, however, be the most meaningless unless it is backed up with an indication of how awareness shifts will be judged to fail or succeed. For example, would a shift of 5 per cent in an awareness score on a tracking study be sufficient to equate to success, or is a 50 per cent increase to be expected? Many companies erroneously assume that the nebulous concept of awareness will somehow always magically convert into something completely different, such as sales. If sales are the objective, state it, and don't confuse it with awareness.

Awareness is often the first stage in communication if a new brand is being launched. In the case of much public sector or health education advertising, raising awareness is the main objective, e.g. AIDS information, the dangers of smoking, etc. Without the basic platform of awareness there is nothing to build a communication plan upon and to direct future actions. Existing and successful brands often have high awareness, hence this would be an inappropriate objective to set. However, some existing brands in a highly competitive market often find that awareness is very fickle and may need to be constantly 'topped up' to retain brand salience in the market.

It should be remembered that awareness need not always be a positive thing. Some advertising can achieve high awareness scores but for the wrong reasons. The messages can be delivered in a patronising way, the advertisement may look dated or be delivered in an inexpert way or maybe it is just downright annoying!

Alter Perceptions and Attitudes

If brands are to be repositioned or repackaged, advertising is likely to be part of the mix to ensure that consumers change how they think about a brand and how they will react to it in the future. A well-documented example of advertising which helped change the perception of a product is Lucozade. From a sick room product of recent history it was repackaged and repositioned as an 'energy' drink. Advertising featuring Daley Thompson, then an Olympic Pentathlete, helped transform the fortunes of this ageing brand. The brand has apparently continued to be successful in the market by building on and developing this new position. It is now seen as a youth cult product with close associations with 'club culture'. This is a brand that has definitely travelled a great perceptual and attitudinal distance.

It is often the case that advertising on its own cannot fulfil this objective. It is likely that many other things, such as pack design, outlets stocking, etc., need to be seen to change at the same time to effect a changed perception and attitude towards a brand.

Create Desires

Advertising is often given a great deal of bad press because 'it makes people want something they don't need'. This does advertising a major disservice. Consumers are not stupid. In reality it is extremely difficult to fool them into buying a brand they neither want nor need. What advertising can do is to tap into latent desires and bring them to the fore to effect a positive response towards the advertised brand. For example, many people have the desire to be wealthy, but they realise that short of winning the lottery they are highly unlikely to achieve this ambition. Compensation can be sought to display some of the outward trappings of wealth that may allude to the fact that they are more wealthy than they are by purchasing luxury goods such as perfume, malt whisky, jewellery, cosmetics or designer label goods. Advertising underpins the so-called exclusivity and cachet of these products and thus hypes their desirability in the eyes of some individuals. For some this may seem immoral or even downright ridiculous, but such advertising underpins and supports a billion dollar industry across the world.

Desires need not always be so selfishly driven. Many consumers have the desire to generate their own 'feel good factor' through contributing to charities. Advertising for charitable organisations helps channel such desires by resulting in donations to a charity of the consumers' choice.

Provide Reassurance

Some advertising will seek to reassure consumers that they have been wise in their past purchasing patterns and should continue in their loyalty towards a brand, as they have obviously made the right decision. Thus, much car advertising, whilst having a primary objective of attracting new purchasers, also works in a more subtle way to reassure existing owners of the brand in question that they have bought a 'good car' and would hence also consider re-purchase of that brand at some time in the future.

Remind

In crowded FMCG markets, the objectives of much of the advertising is to keep a brand 'top of mind' . This advertising is akin to the voice in the wilderness calling, 'don't forget me, I'm still here, keep on buying me please!' As distinctions between brands become harder to articulate, this objective is frequently used a means of helping to establish loyalty and to keep consumers coming back for more of the same. They know what the brand is about, what it offers and that it remains unchanged. The advertising needs to prompt the consumer to put the brand in question into their shopping trolley rather than an own label or competitive equivalent.

Give Reasons for Buying

For some brands there may be developments or new insights that will provide new or different reasons why a consumer should purchase one brand in favour of another. Advertising is a great tool to explain the reasons, be they rational or emotional, why this product should be purchased. Assuming that the reasons stated are relevant and motivating to the consumer, the chance of a purchase being made are increased. For example, in the world of disposable nappies, which apparently are in a state of constant innovation and improvement, the role of advertising is largely to keep the consumer informed of the latest version of the brands that are now on the shelves. These upgrades inevitably give a superior performance in comparison with its predecessor or the competition.

Consolidate a Position and Protect against the Competition

It takes much effort and expense to establish brands and their role in the marketplace. Much advertising for established and successful brands is to reinforce this position and keep it alive in the perception of its consumers. For advertising to do this year in year out, it is tempting to run and rerun proven advertising. This can work for some brands, but for the majority they have to keep the advertising fresh, challenging and innovative whilst still being true to the brand's established positioning. Consolidation and protection are often cited as advertising objectives for established brands in extremely competitive markets.

Demonstrate

It may be important to show and tell what a brand is capable of doing. For some product categories this is a vital part of the communication, as it is the only way that consumers can be given permission to believe in your brand. The power tool and DIY field are perfect examples of this. A drill needs to be seen doing something even though we know what it does. To take the advertising to its logical conclusion, consumers want to see the end benefit of drilling the holes, i.e. the immaculately transformed interior of a 'des res'.

Generate Enquiries

As part of integrated communication campaigns, much advertising now carries some form of response mechanism, usually a telephone number or an e-mail address. This serves many purposes, the most obvious being to gauge the effectiveness of the advertising. This data can also be useful for database building that could be used in future direct marketing campaigns.

Increase Traffic

During holiday periods there is always an influx of certain types of advertising. It is largely targeted to give consumers something to do with the free time they have on their hands. This could involve visiting their local DIY outlet for materials or provide information on a theme park to take their family to. Its objective is straightforward – get bodies through shop doorways or turnstiles to generate sales.

The list of potential advertising objectives could go on and on. The rationale for listing only some of these objectives is two-fold: often there is an overlap between potential objectives, hence the definitive objective must be spelled out clearly and succinctly. Secondly, the more limited the advertising objectives are, the clearer the communication of the finished advertising is likely to be.

In an ideal world, only one objective should be selected. In reality, marketing staff often fall back into the reassurance of providing 'primary' and 'secondary' communication objectives. It is permissible, and it happens everyday in marketing departments around the globe. Experience shows that this approach makes marketing departments feel better, but it won't necessarily result in better advertising. Some of the most successful advertising takes on one advertising task at a time. There is a lesson for all marketing personnel: *shopping lists never result in great advertising.* However, clear thinking that prioritises advertising objectives to single out the one with most potential for the brand in the marketplace will.

What do we want Advertising to Communicate?

At the heart of most successful advertising is the communication of a brand benefit that truly has meaning and is of relevance to the target audience. There are potentially many different benefits that can be attributed to any given brand. It is often difficult to pinpoint the single benefit that will be the most motivating. The benefit selected should signal genuine understanding of consumer behaviour and perceptions of the brand as it now is or how it is desired for it to be positioned in the future. These consumer insights are critical to create relevant and motivating brand differentiators that can be communicated in advertising. Isolating the benefit is most frequently done through the careful use of qualitative research. The methodologies of this research technique will be discussed in detail in Chapter 3.

1.3 UNDERSTANDING BENEFITS AND INSIGHT

These two areas are worthy of separate and detailed discussion, because if they are not understood the advertising may fail. These are the two areas of communication that can potentially provide a sustainable competitive advantage for a brand. While neither concept is new, insight is currently being hailed as something to provide a further competitive edge in advertising development.

Benefits

"Customers don't buy products, they seek to acquire benefits." Behind this statement lies the basic principle of successful advertising. Benefits for product/services can be found in any area of the marketing mix:

- product;
- price;
- place;
- promotion.

The motivation to purchase does not just come out of features or attributes but by the benefit that those attributes bring with them.

The difference between benefits and features is not just a question of semantics. Many companies fall into the trap of thinking of their products as a series of features without thinking what those features mean to the customer. The customer may be unable to translate the benefit that the features deliver, so it makes sense that we should always communicate this clearly.

To ensure that marketing staff does not fall into the 'feature trap', it is always useful to use the phrase 'which means that' to link the features with a benefit. For example:

- 'Wishy Washy' washing up liquid has a mild formulation, *which means that* it is kind to your hands.
- Acme bearings have a unique titanium coating *which means that* they last twice as long as the competition's.

Benefit Analysis

It is wise to take time to fully appraise the benefits you can potentially offer your customer. To help define which benefit or benefits should be talked about in advertising, list all brand features and link them with the benefit. Such analysis can result in isolating many different forms of benefits, such as:

- *Standard benefits.* Basic benefits that may be neither unique nor special.
- *Double benefits.* A single benefit that could be interpreted differently by different markets, e.g. 50 per cent extra pack brings a value benefit to the end user and a faster stock turnover for the retailer.
- *Company benefits*. Oftentimes a customer is buying more than a simple product – they are buying into a relationship with your company. Loyalty programmes are keen to develop and exploit such benefits.
- *Differential benefits.* These are potentially the most potent, as they set your product apart form the competition and enhance its chance of success in the marketplace.

Once the potential areas of benefit have been isolated, their relative appeal should be assessed with the end consumer via qualitative research.

Rosser Reeves, an American psychologist, coined the term 'unique selling proposition' (USP) to explain this benefit encapsulation in advertising communication. Benefit communication is an extremely powerful and enduring weapon in successful advertising campaigns. As markets become increasingly competitive and products are less differentiated, the need for motivating benefits has never been greater.

What Makes Up a Benefit?

A benefit can derive from any area of the marketing mix. For any given benefit to succeed, it should fulfil the following criteria:

- emanate directly from the brand or the experience gained from interacting with it;
- be believable;

- be original;
- signal genuine understanding of consumer needs and motivations;
- be tangible in a rational or an emotional way.

1.4 RATIONAL VERSUS EMOTIONAL BENEFITS

Benefits can be either *rational* or *emotional*. Neither is right or wrong, rather, the choice is dependent on:

- the nature of the product;
- the environment in which it competes;
- the dynamics of the market;
- consumer attitudes.

Rational Benefits

These appeal to reason and offer something to the consumer that is tangible.

Advantages:
- Easy for the consumer to understand.
- Firmly anchored in the product or service.
- Easier to develop.

Disadvantages:
- Can be difficult to protect due to competitive pressure.
- May need to resort to superlatives, which can undermine integrity, e.g. claiming your product is now even bigger, etc.
- Can be one-dimensional and hence creatively limiting.
- May be inappropriate for many product categories.

Emotional Benefits

These are far less tangible and often difficult to be articulated in an entirely logical way. They provide a kind of emotional bond between the consumer and the brand.

Advantages:
- Often a unique territory.
- Enables the development of an emotional bond with the consumer.
- Less vulnerable to competitive attack.
- Often 'multidimensional', enabling creative scope.

Disadvantages:
- Often difficult to isolate.
- Can be too obtuse and alienate the consumer.

There is a continuum between the rational and the emotional which offers much scope for advertisers to precisely define their territory, making this area their own by consistently exploiting it. Once this specific territory is found, it provides the means of differentiating a brand from the competition. This is sometimes referred to as a *competitive advantage* or a *sustainable competitive advantage* (SCA).

Some companies split out rational and emotional benefits for brands. The danger in doing this is that it may become confusing to decide which benefit should be communicated. An uncomfortable compromise can sometimes result when this mix of benefits becomes artificially shoe horned together. For example, a rational benefit for a premium blended whisky could be its *smooth taste delivery* due to its unique blend of malt and grain whiskies. The emotional benefit for this same brand could be the *reassurance* that when serving this whisky to guests they will appreciate your fine taste in selecting such a prestigious brand.

The dangers of including both these benefits with equal weight becomes immediately apparent because two different, albeit vaguely related, stories will need to be told. Such complexities further decrease the chances of producing clear, single-minded advertising, since two benefits already exist. Decisions must be made to find the single most motivating benefit. Some companies overcome this problem by having two different advertising approaches, one to support each benefit, be it rational or emotional. This is an expensive option and can run the risk of neither benefit being given enough weight to achieve effective communication and could cause confusion as the consumer remains unclear about what the brand stands for.

In the United Kingdom, Fairy Liquid has historically been supported with two advertising approaches that give rationally-based benefits. The benefit of *'mildness'* is communicated with the 'little girls/boys' campaign which explains how soft mummy's hands are despite washing mountains of dishes. The partner campaign communicated a *'mileage'* benefit about how long the bubbles lasted and the product performed despite washing the aforementioned mountains of dishes.

In addition to isolating benefits, additional communication is often needed to provide further explanation why the benefit in question can be justified or be given permission to be believed. This is often referred to as the 'support' or the 'reason why' in advertising terminology. This will be discussed in greater detail in Chapter 7.

Isolating a relevant benefit most frequently occurs due to insights being made that elevate the mundane to greater heights to be motivating benefits. In advertising parlance this is the one that 'hits the hot button'!

What is Insight?

There has been much hype and discussion recently in marketing departments and advertising agencies about 'insight', but what exactly do people mean by this and has a recent discovery been made to help us achieve better and more successful advertising?

The dictionary definition of insight does little to help explain the nature of this terminology and its potential use when developing advertising. *The Concise Oxford Dictionary* defines it as "penetration (into character, circumstances, etc.) with the understanding". By my definition, an insight is a fundamental truth that exists about your brand and helps to differentiate it from the competition in a way that the consumer can understand, relate to and ideally buy into as the way in which they view your brand now and in the future. As with a benefit, it will help to give a brand a sustainable competitive advantage.

Unlike a benefit, however, insight doesn't necessarily need to emanate directly from the product. It may relate more to how a product is used, talked about or seen to behave in the competitive context, etc. This is not a totally new concept, but rather, it is a redefinition and refinement of an older advertising maxim: that of defining the 'fundamental truth in your product'.

Like benefits, insights are usually pinpointed through the use of qualitative research to probe consumer understandings and perceptions. They are less commonly stumbled upon during the course of creative development by either client or agency. The marketing and advertising personnel responsible for a brand are often too close to see 'the wood from the trees', know too much about the brand or there may even be 'hidden agendas' which can cloud innovative thinking. Methodologies for isolating insights will be discussed in more detail in Chapter 6.

When brands are repositioned it is often an appropriate time to re-examine the benefits that are communicated to check if there are any insights that may give the advertising an 'edge' to optimise its effect.

Informed observation of the advertising scene in the recent past shows that there are many instances when insights have been used to help provide strategic focus and a resultant competitive edge.

Galaxy Chocolate was positioned in the early 1980s as a 'sharing bar'. The advertising featured large bars of chocolate which were passed amongst groups of people in various scenarios, wherein each snapped off a few squares and passed it on to their neighbour. On the face of it this seems a reasonable positioning and marketing strategy. No other manufacturer had a positioning for block chocolate like this at the time, and as it featured a bigger bar, there should be an increase in the volume sold as consumption switched from small to big bars.

The information on insight, which was likely to have been gained from qualitative research, is missing from all of these assumptions. I suspect that it highlighted that this advertising approach totally alienated Galaxy's core user base, women. In reality, how women choose to eat their chocolate bears no similarity to how eating chocolate was portrayed in this 'sharing' advertising. Women would prefer to eat their chocolate in solitude; it is their personal and private moment of indulgence. This solitude is not depressing or lonely – it is luxurious and in a way deeply sensual. This insight into product usage was incorporated into the re-launch of Galaxy in 1984 and has been a consistent theme of their advertising ever since then. Now the advertising typically shows a woman having her private moment of indulgence. This is the work of insight, not the brand benefit. The brands benefit derives from its smooth texture, and hence the phrase: "Why have cotton when you can have silk?"

This is a neat illustration of how an insight can enhance a benefit communication by placing it in a context that consumers immediately relate to. Insights, however, need not always be separate from a brand benefit – it may even be turned into the brand benefit. A brand like Yellow Pages could quite rightly run the risk of always being associated with disasters or when there is a problem to solve. These are negative rather than positive associations. This negativity could potentially have a backlash effect, as in the longer term the brand would forever have negative associations. The very famous and successful advertising which ran for this brand during the 1980s and early 1990s recognised this consumer insight and showed how it could be used " not just for the nasty things...". The "good old Yellow Pages" advertising had much emotional depth and appeared to be extremely successful and much loved. Indeed, J R Hartley, featured in one of the advertising approaches in pursuit of his book on fly fishing, has almost become a national institution!

The importance of insight should not be overlooked, and in the current marketing scenario for many brands that compete on the basis of offering similar benefits, it is often insight that provides a unique and sustainable competitive positioning. Insights can thus help define a motivating brand benefit or bring an extra dimension to advertising communication that ensures it breaks through the clutter of competing messages.

SUMMARY

In summary, to ensure that the advertising you produce is excellent as opposed to mediocre it is essential that:

- The advertising objectives are absolutely clear. Be as single-minded as possible.
- A single-minded benefit is communicated either rationally, emotionally or some point in between.
- Any relevant insights into brand usage, perceptions, etc. have been understood to provide a competitive advantage.

Chapter 2
Starting the Advertising Development Process

Of all the communication tools available, advertising has the reputation of being the most effective, albeit one of the most expensive options available to promote a company's products, services or brands. Before leaping into this expensive process of developing an advertising campaign, it is prudent to reflect on where advertising fits into the practice of responsible marketing planning.

Too often, it is naïvely assumed that by merely fixing or changing the advertising, the ills of a product, service or brand can be magically transformed overnight. The process of planning and developing advertising should come at the end of a long chain of marketing thinking and planning. Advertising is the culmination and realisation of the marketing plan; hence, it should always be the last thing to be developed if the marketing department is doing its job correctly.

There is a fundamental truth about advertising: everyone loves it, wants to be involved in its development, is a 'natural expert' on it and usually finds it to be a fun part of their job. Thus, there is always the temptation to rush to start developing advertising because it is an enjoyable thing to do.

Many people falsely believe that any unresolved issues in marketing planning and communication strategy will somehow 'sort themselves out' during the process of advertising development. Sometimes they do but more often they don't, resulting in poorly thought-out marketing and communication strategic directions for brands, and ultimately in failed communication plans and wasted marketing budget.

By rushing this process it is too easy to forget about the planning and thinking which needs to be done to make sure that communication is going to be optimised. To get the most out of a communication and advertising campaign, a logical process should be followed to ensure that the thinking has been done before the implementation of communication plans.

1. Redefine the role of the product you wish to advertise within the terminology of the *marketing concept*.
2. Conduct a *strategic trawl*.
3. Consider the role of other communication tools by taking an *integrated* approach to communication planning.
4. Finally, develop a *brief* for the agency to start the creative development process. A thorough brief should consist of a Brand Essence Statement, Brand Positioning Statement, Communication Mix Statement and Creative Brief (see Chapter 7).

Many companies erroneously start the development of their advertising campaign with the last point, briefing the agency. When this happens, it is likely that great advertising could be developed, but it may fail completely in the eyes of the client. This failure may not be the fault of the advertising agency. They may have been wrongly briefed because the client has not understood how his product fits into the marketing concept, what his customers' wants and needs currently are or how his product can fulfil these wants and needs. The development of advertising should always be at the end of this strategic development process. This 'back to basics' approach will ensure that the end communication will be as focused as possible to enhance its chances of success.

How Does Advertising Fit Into the Marketing Concept?

This section serves as a summary of the marketing process and as a reminder of the other areas of marketing planning which must be clarified prior to developing advertising.

There are many worthy answers to the question 'what is marketing?' In essence, a company that claims to be marketing-oriented places the needs and wants of its customers at the very centre of its business decisions.

There have been many definitions of marketing. The Chartered Institute of Marketing defines it as "the management process responsible for identifying, anticipating and satisfying customer requirements profitably". In layman's terms, marketing is the art of "selling goods which don't come back to customers who do".

Marketing is also erroneously limited to the four P's – product, price, promotion and place. A broader look at the total marketing concept should always be borne in mind when preparing communication plans. The use of communication tools and advertising in particular is the end of the marketing process. It should never be the starting point, or else it is likely that there will be mistakes made as the broader marketing context may have been overlooked.

2.1 THE MARKETING CONCEPT

The stages in taking a marketing-led approach are as follows:
- portfolio positioning;
- competitive strategy;
- target consumer segment;
- competitive advantage;
- focused marketing mix;
- product, price, promotion, place.

Portfolio Positioning

A portfolio can be a single product, service or brand or, as is the case for many FMCG companies, groups of brands, all of which have to be 'managed' for both their individual brand and the company's long-term health.

It is absolutely essential that the individual roles of brands within the portfolio are understood and agreed upon, e.g. are they being managed for cash, managed for growth, retaining status quo, etc. This must be decided on upfront, as it will determine the shape and nature of the rest of the marketing plan. Individual brands within the portfolio are likely to play different roles to provide a balance. If too many brands are playing similar roles it will be problematic to manage them. For example, if all are being managed for growth it will be expensive to finance. Similarly, if they are being managed for cash this may reduce the brand and company's health in the longer term.

In simplistic terms, responsible portfolio management finds the optimum balance between managing the existing established elements of the portfolio for cash to finance the rising stars for growth. In this way, cash flow is retained whilst ensuring the longer term health of a company.

Competitive Strategy

The predetermined portfolio strategy will determine what competitive strategy will be adopted. If managing for growth, it is likely to be very aggressive, and if managing for cash, it will be more passive and reactive.

Target Consumer Segment

The core target must be fully understood in as many ways as possible to find out what makes them 'tick'. Without such knowledge, it will be impossible to ensure that the given brands will be of interest or relevance to the target consumer. The dimensions which are commonly used to understand consumers are demographics, psychographics/lifestyle and understanding the complexities of consumer behaviour patterns.

Competitive Advantage

For a brand to succeed in the longer term and to be perceived as a brand, it should have a 'sustainable competitive advantage'. A competitive advantage differentiates brands from the competition and sets it apart. The most usual way of differentiating brands is by ensuring that they deliver a benefit which may be rational or emotional. A competitive advantage can also be found by understanding any insights which may exist that relate to the brand, such as how consumers use it, perceive it, etc. (see Chapter 1 for more detail on this). The fit between the target consumer and a competitive advantage is the positioning that a brand will adopt in the marketplace.

Focused Marketing Mix

A brand's marketing mix can be determined by planning its role in the portfolio and its competitive strategy, and by understanding the target and the competitive advantage the brand is to deliver. The decision that is made on the product format, price, the distribution channels (place) and how it is promoted will largely be determined by all of the thinking that has already taken place.

If this flow of logic is not followed, it is possible that there will be fundamental flaws in the marketing mix, e.g. wrong price, an inappropriate product that delivers a meaningless benefit, a product stocked in inappropriate distribution channels, inappropriately used promotional tools, an irrelevant advertising message.

Applying this flow of logic for any given product or service results in the development of the marketing strategy, i.e. the plan that will put into place the necessary elements to achieve the growth rate, profitability, etc.

Advertising is only one of the potential communication/promotional tools that could be employed, and is therefore one of the very last things that should be resolved when marketing products or services.

If the quality of marketing thinking is sound, the advertising positioning will be easier to resolve. The translation of this desired positioning into a relevant and forceful advertising idea should also be easier providing that clear, single-minded direction is given to the advertising agency.

2.2 CONDUCT A STRATEGIC TRAWL

Having decided the role of the product or service within the marketing concept, it is now time to take the development process on to the next stage by conducting a strategic trawl.

Different companies and company cultures have their own language and paperwork that will not necessarily be called a 'strategic trawl'. This is my umbrella terminology that explains the depth of understanding that is needed about any market prior to the development of a formal advertising brief.

Within the field of marketing there is an awful lot of jargon, and there is always the temptation to give simple concepts very fancy titles. It may make us feel that this makes marketing an extremely intellectual practice, but it can often cause confusion when one misunderstands and misinterprets the language.

The approach that I recommend is not unique. Many clients that I have worked with find being rational and easy to understand an extremely useful way to help them order their thoughts to ensure that they genuinely understand the role that advertising and other communication tools should fulfil in their communication programmes.

A strategic trawl provides the basic information that is used to start the development of any proposed communications. It puts into words or pictures the intentions of the marketing strategy that result from understanding the product role within the marketing concept discussed earlier in this chapter. It is the 'fuel' that drives the marketing strategy.

A thorough strategic trawl will ensure that the communication plan is consistent with the overall marketing objectives and has the benefit of forcing thinking 'through the line' to ensure that all communications are consistent. It ensures that all the facts that relate to the brand are explored. On completion there should not be any unanswered questions.

Remember that any information unearthed in the strategic trawl is not a written in stone – it should be an evolving entity that is constantly adapting within the context of the competitive environment.

A strategic trawl seeks to provide answer to the following questions:

- What?
- Who is our target customer?
- Why do we need to communicate with them?
- Where should our communication be seen?
- When?
- How should we be communicating with our target?
- How much?

What?

- What are we selling: a lifestyle experience, a solution to stain removal, peace of mind, etc.? It is vital that you are absolutely clear about what your product or service actually delivers as opposed to what you believe it delivers.
- What is the overall marketing objective we wish to achieve: penetration (getting everyone to use the product), trial (get new users to try for first time), loyalty (recognise we have a loyal customer base so hang on to them), etc.? Advertising can often only do one job at a time, so prioritise the marketing objective that is the most important to you.

- What response do we want from customers? How do they think and behave towards us?
- What is the message we want to convey to them?
- What are the priorities in communication? Often many things need to be said; therefore, there is a need to prioritise. Beware of trying to say too much, as there is a danger of nothing being communicated if the message is too long or complicated.
- What don't we want to convey? Be aware of sensitive areas that could have a negative impact.

Who is our Target Customer?
- Where do they live?
- How old are they?
- What lifestage are they at?
- How much disposable income do they have?
- What makes them tick (psychographics/lifestyle)?
- Which media do they use? Knowing this helps isolate channels of communication, which is particularly helpful when developing media plans. This is discussed in greater detail in Chapter 11.
- How do they feel about us – good, bad or indifferent? How do we want this to change?
- Are there any other ways of finding these people (geodemographics)?

Why do we Need to Communicate with Them?
- What are they doing now? What brands or alternatives are they currently buying? Are they lapsed, current or new users?
- How do we want their behaviour to change?
- Do we want their perception of us to change? How do we want them to think of us in the future?

Where should our Communication be Seen?

- Which tools are thought to be the most effective in achieving our objectives, and which are impacted by budget? We also need to consider the potential coverage of our target and their CPTs (cost per thousand).
- Look at which tools have worked well in the past. Don't be afraid of recycling proven ideas, but beware of becoming too complacent.
- Look at the competition – what do we think is working well for them? Look outside the immediate competitive environment for new ideas.
- Where do we want to be seen? Some communication tools may be inconsistent with our desired positioning.

When should our Communications be Seen?

- What is the most appropriate timing for our communications?
- Is there seasonality in the market? If so, do we follow it or counter it?
- Are there other promotional activities that we have to fit in with, either within the company, the division or in comparison to the competition?
- Do budgeting limits restrict the timing if we can only afford 'cheaper' times of the year when using some media?

How should we be Communicating with our Target?

- How do we talk to these people, and what is the tone of voice (e.g. knowledgeable, assuming, educational, etc.)?
- How complex is the message? The simpler the better – prioritise communication objectives.
- What sort of language should we use – are there any appropriate buzz words? Is this consistent with the tone? This is a very judgmental area, so it is often necessary to use research to check that tone is correct.

How Much?

There is never enough budget to do everything, therefore:

- We need a contingency plan for minimum versus maximum, especially if budgets are not guaranteed.

- Decisions need to be made to prioritise amongst the tools that impact on where, how and when the communications occur.

During the preparation of a strategic trawl, it cannot be emphasised enough that the more single-minded and focused you are, the clearer your resultant brief for the advertising agency will be. Experience has proven that clear, single-minded briefs produce better and more effective advertising. This is discussed in greater detail in Chapter 7.

There is always the temptation to include as much information as possible in a strategic trawl for fear of leaving something out. This approach is totally wrong and indicates that more work needs to be done to clarify, simplify and make the communication strategy as single-minded as possible. The first draft is likely to be too comprehensive, therefore continually review and revise it until it is clear and focused.

2.3 CHOOSING BETWEEN COMMUNICATION TOOLS

After conducting a strategic trawl, the next step is to decide which of the communication tools available are the most appropriate to use. The budget will help shape the communications plan, and the larger the budget, the more complex the planning process becomes as there are far more options available to select from. It should be noted that there is no such thing as a perfect communication tool. At this stage in the planning process, only broad decisions need to be made in shaping the communication plan. A refined list of selected tools is part of the Communication Mix Statement, which is discussed in Chapter 7.

These pros and cons are in no way intended to be exhaustive, but rather, are meant to underpin the fact that a lot of judgement is often needed when deciding which communication tools should be included or excluded in an integrated communications plan.

A brief explanation of the tools and their relative pros and cons is as follows.

Advertising

Advertising is any paid-for communication which appears in a recognised media. The objectives of any given advertisement will vary depending on the product or service being promoted. The main media that are used are television, press, outdoor, radio and cinema. The characteristics and pros and cons of these media are discussed in greater detail in Chapter 10.

Pros:
- Intrusive.
- Proven track record.
- Most potent tool to change attitudes and behaviour.
- Often has an immediate effect.
- Part of popular culture.
- Results often quantifiable, providing that appropriate data/intelligence is available.
- Able to target different segments through selective use of media.
- Creatively flexible.
- Provides a sustainable competitive advantage.
- Provides leverage to get product listed/stocked.
- Motivates sales force.
- Lower cost (media and production) options are available in some media (e.g. local radio).

Cons:
- Expensive, both media and production.
- Wastage through some channels as they only reach a broad target (e.g. terrestrial television).
- Many media are transitory, making it difficult to register message.
- Many media are crowded, therefore it is difficult to achieve stand-out (e.g. tabloid press).
- Lengthy process to plan and develop campaigns, making it difficult/problematic to use tactically.
- Fragmenting media market makes it less reliable to target certain segments.

Direct Marketing

This is a growing field that is comprised of several techniques:

- Direct mail – consumer and business to business.
- Media based direct response adverts – television, press and radio.
- Telemarketing – in and out-bound calls.
- Mail order and direct selling.
- Door to door.
- New media: Internet, CD-ROM, multimedia kiosks, video on demand, interactive television.

Pros:
- Precise targeting.
- In theory, best prospects can be isolated.
- Expenditure is channelled effectively, therefore there is less waste.
- Enables a depth of information to be delivered.
- Immediately accountable – some tools provide immediate feedback on efficacy (e.g. direct response advertising).
- Campaigns can be as large or small as is affordable.
- Discrete, therefore able to test alternative options to maximise learning.

Cons:
- Consumer hostility to some tools (e.g. direct mail, telemarketing).
- Can be expensive (e.g. quality mailshot £2.00 per mail out).
- Some techniques not immediate, therefore require longer term investment (e.g. some direct mail campaigns).
- Control may be reduced with some tools (e.g. out-bound telemarketing).
- Quality of external databases cannot always be 100 per cent guaranteed.
- Internal database management can require investment and specialised skills to keep it efficient.

Sales Promotion

There are an almost infinite number of sales promotions available, such as competitions, multi-link purchases, price reductions, free gifts, reduced price gifts, money-off coupons, loyalty schemes, cross promotions, personalities, interest free credit, etc.

The recent trends in the development of sales promotion techniques have led to the distinction of long and short-term promotions. Short-term promotions are used in a more tactical manner to provide alterations in behaviour over a limited period of time, e.g. money-off coupons. The long-term promotions are used in a more strategic manner and have a longer proposed period of operation, e.g. loyalty schemes.

The former schemes are much cheaper, flexible and easier to plan. The latter require considerably more investment and commitment.

Pros:

- Many are quick and cheap to set up in comparison with other communication tools.
- Costs are more controllable.
- If 'novel' it can have a disproportionate effect.
- Adds news-value.
- Flexible – can be as large or as small as is affordable.
- Results often quantifiable, assuming that data/intelligence gathering is done before and after usage.
- Trade visibility.
- Attention grabber at point of sale.
- Provides short-term sales boost.

Cons:

- Impact limited due to cynicism/boredom on the part of the consumer.
- Malredemption (coupons).
- Can become expected norm and reduce impact (e.g. multi-purchase, loyalty schemes).
- Many are inappropriate to promotional/marketing strategy.

Starting the Advertising Development Process

- Many are short-term.
- Complexity and longevity of some promotions can incur consumer ill will.
- Rewards are often seen as not worth the effort.
- Some targets are not responsive to sales promotions, hence will never be reached.
- Can be logistical problems which add to the on-cost (e.g. in/on pack offers).

Public Relations

This is a very broad discipline that is often hard to define exactly and merges with other disciplines. Simply put, public relations (PR) can be defined as being either proactive or reactive. Proactive PR enables more control and influence to be exerted over the medium in question, whereas reactive PR is often referred to more as 'fire-fighting/damage limitation'.

The areas that PR covers include: press relations, consumer relations, internal communications, community relations, liaison with opinion formers/lobby groups, etc.

Pros:

- Can be relatively inexpensive to achieve high exposure levels.
- Often seen as third party endorsement, hence has more weight/authority.
- Gives an opportunity to achieve exposure in media often inaccessible via any other tool (e.g. nightly news, front page of a newspaper).
- Works in a less obvious/intrusive way, which appeals to certain segments.

Cons:

- Often difficult to control what is said (e.g. requires specialists to guide editorial comments, etc.).
- Relies heavily on strength of personal relationships to have an effect.
- Often difficult to quantify effectiveness.
- May lack visibility.

Sponsorship

This is any paid-for association with an event or programme. Sponsorship deals are available that cover a wide range of events and media. Sponsorship has historically been important in sports and the arts, but now it is gaining further prominence with the advent of media sponsorship in general and television sponsorship in particular.

Pros:

- Opportunity to acquire values unique to the sponsorship opportunity.
- Can reach specific targets to minimise wastage.
- Can complement/enhance product or service.
- Gives standout as some sponsorship opportunities are still perceived as 'novel'.
- Can provide protection from competitive activity.
- Provides a focus around which other promotions can be structured.

Cons:

- Often difficult to demonstrate effect in the short-term.
- Some sponsorship opportunities inappropriate.
- Often difficult to find 'perfectly matched' sponsorship opportunities.
- Sponsorship overload in some fields (e.g. motor sports).

Exhibitions

Again, this is a broad discipline that can be used to good effect to target certain consumers, trade and even for internal communication. The scale and size of the exhibition/event will largely determine the degree of investment which is required to design and build stands and to staff a stand. The efficient and effective use of exhibitions is more complex than may be initially thought.

For some categories of business, the use of exhibitions in conjunction with PR forms a key plank to many marketing strategies. For example, many car launches are timed to coincide with the Frankfurt or

UK motor shows. For other companies their use may be totally inappropriate.

> **Pros:**
> - Provides interface with DMU.
> - 'Live' product experience.
> - 'Larger than life' experience, which aids memorability.
> - Part of database generation exercise.
> - Attracts many customers.
>
> **Cons:**
> - Can be expensive to design, build and run.
> - Often difficult to quantify immediate effect.
> - Some wastage, as not all people visiting a stand may ultimately purchase.
> - Many have a very short life.

Merchandising

This communication tool covers all material and services produced to support a product or service. Its objectives are usually to give the product/service extra presence or to provide information that will help effect a sale. Effective merchandising will ensure that any product or service is in the right place at the right time, with enough support material available to effect a sale. It covers such diverse areas as point-of-sale material, brochures, sales force literature, etc.

> **Pros:**
> - Provides stand out at point-of-sale.
> - Gives a depth of information (e.g. brochures).
> - May give leverage to stock.

Cons:

✔ Usage not always guaranteed.

✔ May be misused, which can reflect badly on product/service.

✔ Often labour-intensive to provide/maintain.

✔ Efficacy difficult to quantify.

2.4 INTEGRATED COMMUNICATIONS

Having discussed that there are a large number of communication tools available, the next stage in the planning process is to determine which tools are likely to be the most appropriate to use and include them in a Communication Mix Statement (see Chapter 7).

Advertising is often judged to be the most important tool in terms of the budget allocated to it and its efficacy. As it is often not the only tool that is used, it is essential that there is a consistency in strategic approach and resultant executions across all tools. It is vital to remember that the target consumer doesn't necessarily distinguish between messages received from individual tools since they only see the big picture. Planning must be geared towards this integrated approach prior to writing briefs. This planning process is at the heart of successful integrated communication.

All communication, be it a sales promotion or a piece of point-of-sale, should be consistent in its approach. However, it should be noted that an advertising idea is often the pivot and core from which the strategic and creative direction for the other tools are developed.

Several factors have coincided, resulting in marketers re-examining their approach to the use of communication tools in a more integrated way. Historically, communication tools have been treated as separate disciplines that operate separately in the marketplace. This separation of techniques and personnel responsible for developing them exacerbated the belief that they work differently and in isolation.

It is now recognised that techniques impinge and have an effect on each other, both positively and negatively. All techniques should be developed to form a consistent communication strategy and as far as possible they should be harnessed to work together to gain the benefits of synergy through their combined effect. Such a change in thinking has had a great impact on how both clients and agencies approach the development of creative work.

The factors that have acted together to drive a move towards integrated communication are as follows.

- *Media Fragmentation.* On a worldwide basis, there are more and more media available to carry advertising messages. Some advertisers worry that the plethora of media makes it difficult to reliably predict who will be viewing a given channel when there are more than 250 to choose from. This has led to the growth of disciplines, such as direct marketing, that claim to target consumers more reliably and with less wastage.

- *Media Globalisation.* The advent of satellite-based television has resulted in the birth of the 'global village'. Only the Arctic and Antarctica remain untouched by a satellite footprint. Star TV covers 43 countries and more than 3,000 million people – the Buddhist in Bangkok receives the same programming as the Catholic in the Philippines. Such factors are driving the move towards consistent product positioning across larger markets. The need for communication tools to work together on a broad scale has never been greater.

- *Budget Restraints.* Budgets (and marketing budgets in particular) are not bottomless pits, therefore the most effective deployment of communication budgets should be sought. Budgetary pressure should encourage innovative thinking on how communication tools can be integrated to maximise their effect.

- *Consumer Sophistication.* In more developed markets, consumers understand how the communication mix operates. They can be critical, and indeed may become confused if different communication tools provide conflicting messages.

- *Technological Developments.* The advent of all types of computer-based technology has enabled the development of communication tools as diverse as the Internet, direct mail and telemarketing. Since it is easy and in some cases more economically sound to use these tools, it is essential that the messages they carry remain consistent.

- *Agency Structures.* Advertising agencies have been quick to respond to these developments in communication by becoming integrated themselves. Many agencies now have separate profit centres offering services such as direct marketing, sales promotion, PR, etc. The theory is that such integrated agencies are in a better position to develop truly integrated campaigns, as they are able to control and influence the nature of the communication irrespective of the tool being used. Integrated agencies are in some cases driving this phenomena.

- **Corporate Philosophy.** Clients are themselves adopting a more integrated approach and are imposing this discipline upon their marketing departments through restructuring.

Integration should thus ensure that there is a consistency in strategic and creative communication with the consumer. As the communication tools should be designed to work together, the result should be that the consumer has a totally consistent and cohesive picture of what the brand stands for and is delivering.

To be able to integrate successfully, brands should operate under a consistent strategy. Developing creative work across all discipline areas in tandem often enhances the integration effect.

It should be noted that individual executions should always be checked back to the original briefing documentation (see Chapter 7 for further details) to check that they are consistent and that they communicate with the consumer as intended. Commonly used research techniques are discussed in Chapter 3.

SUMMARY

If this information gathering and distillation is carried out thoroughly, the result should be a starting point for a cohesive marketing and communication strategy. Such a strategy gives a clear indication of what the brand should be saying and to whom it should be saying it. Clarity of thought is critical in this process. It cannot be emphasised enough that this process should never be rushed through as a mere intellectual exercise. The thinking and understanding gained during this stage of the planning process will result in a firm foundation that the resultant communication plan can build upon.

Chapter 3
Research for Advertising Development

This chapter reviews the main research processes and other types of information that are used in the various planning and development stages that lead up to the production of advertising. The approach is sequential and begins with the brand planning process that sets the marketing objectives for the brand. These in turn define the communication – and within that, advertising – objectives.

Subsequent stages are:

- Research prior to the creative brief to better understand the consumer context, and if necessary research to reappraise the brand positioning.

- Research for creative development to help appraise and develop early advertising ideas.

- Pre-testing research to assess the likely marketplace impact of fully developed advertising.

3.1 RESEARCH AND INFORMATION FOR BRAND MARKETING PLANNING

Put simply, brand marketing planning involves three main activities:

1. *Review* of our brand in its consumer, market and broader socio-economic contexts.

2. *Evaluation* of its current situation: strengths, weaknesses, opportunities and threats.

3. *Formulation* of a realistic set of goals for the brand (consistent with the brand's corporate portfolio role), and specification of the means to achieve them (the brand marketing strategy).

The review activity is based totally on market research and other relevant information.

The Brand Review Process

SOCIAL-ECONOMIC CONTEXT
legislation/"rules"
economic trends
population trends
social trends
technology

MARKET
size
trend (growth/decline)
regionality
seasonality
related markets (i.e. possibly threats)

MARKET COMPETITION
our brand versus competitor brands
SOM*, distribution, ROS*, pricing
trends
nature of competition

THE CONSUMER – BEHAVIOUR
Market
who buys/who doesn't
heavy/medium/light buyers

Brands
brand buyers
heavy/medium/light buyers
loyalty levels

THE CONSUMER – PERCEPTIONS/ATTITUDES
Market
what consumer needs are met?
reasons for heavy/medium/light/non purchase
key consumer segments (consumers with different needs)

Brands
salience/perceptions
differentiated benefits
brand/consumer relationship (strength/nature)

* SOM = share of market
* ROS = rate of sale

Key Elements of the Brand Review Process

- *Socio-economic context.* These are big, fundamental forces that grind away (often out of sight), but can have a powerful impact on consumers and marketplaces, e.g. mass availability of the contraceptive pill in the 1960s, affluent 'grey' (50+) consumers in the 1990s, rise of 'healthy eating'.

- *Our market.* The status, health and direction of our market is of fundamental importance, as is the status of other markets that may threaten indirect competition.

- *Market competition.* We need to know not just what the status of our brand is *vis-a-vis* competitor brands, but also the nature of competition in our market, e.g. brand/advertising-driven versus price/promotion-driven.

- *The consumer.* Most importantly, we need to understand our consumers – how they act and how they think/feel.

We need to understand all of these key elements in respect of our market and the brands within it.

Market Research and Other Information

Brand Review Process	Market Research and Other Information
Socio-economic context	Government/CSO publications Population forecasts *Social Trends* (annual book) Futurology/forecasting organisations (e.g. Henley Centre for Forecasting) Technical journals
Market/market competition	EIU or Mintel (market reviews) AC Nielsen (retail audits) Consumer panels (e.g. Superpanel) Trade press
Consumer behaviour	Consumer panels U & A surveys Loyalty card analysis
Consumer perceptions/attitudes	Qualitative research (focus groups or depth interviews) U & A surveys

	Tracking surveys Consumer satisfaction surveys/product tests

NOTE:
An increasing amount of published information (e.g. national newspaper, trade press) is available online.

Key Research Processes

Consumer Panels

Good for:

1. Understanding brand dynamics (i.e. where a brand's gains are coming from and where its losses are going to).

2. Behavioural indication of brand loyalty (how many purchases a brand gets out of an individual's total market purchases).

Qualitative Research

Good for:

1. Unearthing the full range of (deep-seated) consumer needs/purchase motivations (e.g. need for social recognition).

2. Understanding the nature of the consumer-brand relationship (e.g. parent, friend, faithful servant).

3. Understanding differentiated brand benefits (emotional as well as functional).

U & A/Tracking Surveys

Good for:

1. Measurement of brand salience and consumer perceptions of a brand.

2. Consumer self-assessment of brand loyalty ('loyalty ladders').

3.2 USING THE BRAND REVIEW TO SET BRAND MARKETING OBJECTIVES AND STRATEGY

A typical brand will have:

- a clearly defined (corporate) portfolio role;
- a clearly defined brand 'positioning' (the brand's key functional and/or emotional benefit(s) matched against a specific target consumer group).

The brand review process will highlight opportunities and threats, and will indicate specific courses of action that might be followed to achieve the long-term brand objective (as defined by the brand's portfolio role). For example:

- *Long-term brand role:* cash generator.
- *Brand long-term objective:* maintenance of SOM/margin.
- *Brand review process:* indicates the brand is losing SOM and social relevance among young consumers.
- *Brand marketing objective*: to restore SOM among young consumers.
- *Strategy*: make the brand more contemporary and appealing to young consumers (without alienating older loyalists).

Setting Communication Objectives

Communication objectives should flow simply and naturally from brand objectives/strategy. Communications tools (advertising, PR, promotions, etc.) should be selected on the basis of appropriateness to the task and within an integral framework. Continuting our example:

Communication Objectives

1. To project a more contemporary brand image.
2. To stimulate brand trial/repurchase among young consumers.
3. To reinforce purchasing among older brand loyalists.

Communication Tools

Objective 1: advertising.

Objective 2: advertising/trial generating promotions.

Objective 3: loyalty promotions.

3.3 RESEARCH AND INFORMATION PRIOR TO THE CREATIVE BRIEF

We now have :

- A clear marketing objective and strategy.
- Clear communication objectives.
- The specific role for advertising within the communication program.

Although the key elements are decided upon, there remain two areas where we may need further information:

1. *What specifically do we need to say in our advertising?*

    By this we do not mean the key brand benefit(s), which typically remain constant over long periods of time. However, we might not know how best to express the benefit(s) in a relevant way, or, using our example above, how to express contemporariness.

2. *How do we need to say it?*

    What tone of voice, what language and situations, what style of thought, what style of humour? (These must be appropriate to our target consumer.)

If the depth and quality of information in the brand review is good, we may be able to answer these questions. If we are unable to answer them, we will need to conduct consumer research. Typically, to answer either or both questions, qualitative research (focus groups) will be used. The main advantages of this type of research are:

- Speed/flexibility.
- Precise consumer focus (i.e. groups are representative of the target market).
- Gets close to the consumer: lifestyle, attitudes, language, relationship with the brand/market.

In addition, qualitative research is quite good at unearthing 'consumer insights' – little nuggets of information about the consumer's relationship with the brand that can add authenticity or provide a creative startpoint for advertising executions. The following are a few questions one could ask to discover these consumer insights.

- How do we best express contemporariness and attach it credibly to our brand?
- What is our young target consumer's mindset/lifestyle?
- How will older loyalists respond to brand contemporarisation?

Research Process Example

Method
- 1½ hour duration focus groups.

Sample
- Four groups with 18-25s (two brand users, two non-users).
- Two groups with brand loyalists aged 35-50.

Stimulus Material
- A range of expressions of 'contemporariness' (collage boards, television/film clips).
- Diaries/photos of consumer's 'last week' to prompt discussion of their lifestyle and attitudes among 18-25s.
- Key brand representations for our brand (pack/logo).

Discussion Outline
- Main focus on 18-25s: lifestyle/attitudes; relevant expressions of contemporariness; perceptions of our brand; fit with contemporariness.
- Secondary focus on older loyalists and their response to possible contemporising expressions for the brand.

3.4 RESEARCH TO REAPPRAISE THE BRAND POSITIONING

Although a brand's positioning typically remains fixed for a long time, situations arise where fundamental reappraisal becomes necessary. For example:

- Where a brand's existing positioning is losing relevance in the market.
- Where a brand has been left moribund by management, and a decision is made to try to regenerate it.

In either case, the procedure is similar and is outlined below.

Benefit Generation

1. Review all aspects of the brand to establish possible consumer benefits, both functional and emotional.
2. If necessary, conduct qualitative research with consumers to explore the brand through their eyes and unearth further potential benefits.
3. Assess the benefits 'long list', weed out the weaker candidates and eliminate overlap/duplication.
4. Translate the remaining 'shortlist' benefits into an appropriate format for assessment by consumers in research.

Research Process Example

Typically, the research process will be qualitative, and the brand benefits will be represented by boards. The representation on board may be simple sentences, or some combination of words and visual illustration. However, there is a trade-off to be made.

'Words Only' are the purest expression of a benefit but:
- ✓ they are unexciting;
- ✓ they tend to under-represent emotional benefits.

'Words and Pictures' are:
- more involving/exciting;
- better at expressing emotional benefits;
- however, consumers tend to regard words/pictures as 'advertising' and judge them on the basis of the execution, rather than intrinsic appeal of the benefit.

Guidelines

- Consider your brand – what is the relative importance of functional and emotional benefits?
- Consider your target consumers – are they more rational, or are they more emotional?
- How responsive are your target consumers to words versus pictures?

3.5 RESEARCH FOR CREATIVE DEVELOPMENT

The creative brief has been agreed on, and initial creative ideas have been generated. We now need to know two things:

1. What merit do the creative ideas have?
2. Can they be improved, and if so, how?

Taking the case where a new advertising campaign is being developed, research will typically be used at the stage where one or more campaign ideas with apparent potential have been generated.

Objectives of Research

The objective of research at this stage is to:
- evaluate the potential of the campaign idea(s) against target consumers;
- provide guidelines for optimisation of the most promising idea(s).

Specifically, campaign ideas will be evaluated for:

- **Communication effectiveness:** does the advertising idea adequately convey the key thing we want to communicate about our brand?

- **Creative vehicle effectiveness:** does the creative vehicle (the 'idea') appear to be distinctive/different, and is it impactful and/or involving? ('Impact' will tend to be more important for more rationally-based communications, whereas 'involvement' will tend to be more important for more emotionally-based communications).

- **Executional elements:** are detail executional elements (e.g. choice of a presenter, use of a specific music track) generating an appropriate response and are they felt to be appropriate to the basic 'idea'?

It should be noted that in the case where we are developing new executions for an established campaign, the main focus will be on consumer response to the new execution(s) and their perceived consistency with the overall campaign.

Research Method Example

Qualitative research is typically used because:

- it is good at exploring consumer responses, and understanding the 'why?' behind those responses;
- it is a reasonably accessible/comprehensible process: it is possible for creative people to learn a lot by observing research sessions;
- its flexible, interactive format allows the researcher to respond directly to consumer feedback and explore ways to address problems/issues.

The two most commonly used research methods are the 'focus group' (or group discussion) and the 'depth interview'.

Focus groups are used for speed, cost and the ability to talk to a reasonable number of target consumers within a simple, limited research format. Arguably, focus groups are most appropriate to developing advertising that will be 'consumed' in a 'social' or 'public' way (i.e. the research method 'mimics' the way the advertising will be received in real life).

Depth interviews are used less frequently, largely for reasons of cost and timing (they tend to require more cost and time than focus groups). The strength of the depth interview is its ability to explore individual responses to a piece of communication, uncontaminated by outside influences. As such, the method is appropriate to advertising that is designed to work against individuals in a "non-social" way.

3.6 HOW IS THE ADVERTISING IDEA PRESENTED TO THE CONSUMER?

This is a difficult subject within advertising development research. Ideally, the consumer would be shown finished advertising. However, we are at an early stage in advertising development, and this is clearly not practical. The solution is to represent the proposed advertising by some form of surrogate material. All such materials are inadequate representations, in which trade-offs and compromises are made.

The most typically used representations for television/cinema advertising are:

- *Narrative tape:* an audio tape in which an announcer describes the commercial to someone who hasn't seen it, taking them through it step by step.

- *Soundtrack and key frame boards:* a series of illustrated boards depicting key frames, accompanied by a recorded soundtrack.

- *Animatic:* a rough, cartoon-like rendition of the commercial, complete with soundtrack.

- *Photomatic:* an animatic that uses photo and press clips in place of hand drawings.

The most typically used representations for press/posters are:

- *Rough layouts*: these are hand-drawn representations of the ad. These layouts may be more or less complete, i.e. headline and outline illustration only, or headline and fuller copy and more detailed illustration.

Television/Cinema Advertising

The strength of the narrative tape is that it presents the advertising idea in a simple ("pure") format that does not invite the consumer to "judge" it on executional style/detail. The drawback is that it allows the consumer to invent his own "mind picture" of how the commercial will look, and this may bear no resemblance to what the creative team has in mind.

As one progresses down the list, with each representation becoming more "finished", the trade-off is as follows: the more finished the representation, the greater understanding the researcher has about what the consumer is responding to; however, the more finished the representation, the more likely the consumer is to critique it as "real advertising" (i.e. focusing on executional style, as opposed to the basic creative idea).

It is arguable that soundtrack and key frame boards is the best compromise: it indicates the form/content of the advertising pretty clearly, yet its "rough" finish tends to focus consumers on responding to the "idea" rather than executional style.

Press/Poster Advertising

There is a narrower range of representational material to choose from, which potentially allows brand owners to experiment to find the material that works best for their brand. If the main objective is to evaluate advertising ideas (as opposed to detail copy), a simple representation is probably best.

Creative development research is neither precise nor infallible in its assessment of new creative ideas. However, it is generally felt to be helpful to those involved in developing advertising, and to be less hit and miss than the use of judgement alone. Research of this type tends to be better at some tasks than others.

Research evaluation of:	How effective?
Communication effectiveness	Reasonaly good
Creative vehicle effectiveness	Broad indication only
Executional elements	Reasonably good

3.7 PRE-TESTING

"Pre-testing" is research conducted on advertising prior to exposure to the public in the media. Typically, though not always, finished material is tested. The primary reason for pre-testing is to assess what effect the advertising is likely to have in the marketplace; a second reason is to provide "diagnostic" feedback on how the advertising is working (or not working). Pre-testing is mainly geared to television advertising, though it can be applied to other types. It uses relatively large samples (100+) to ensure statistical robustness.

Assessment of Effect in the Marketplace

There are two broad approaches:
1. Assessment of likely effect on sales ("sales effect").
2. Assessment of likely effect on the brand's standing (perceptions/attachment) among consumers ("brand effect").

The first approach assumes that the primary objective of advertising is to generate an uplift in sales; the second approach assumes that the primary objective of advertising is to sustain a brand's consumer appeal, thereby underpinning long-term sales and margin. Different research processes are used to assess likely "sales effect" and likely "brand effect".

Pre-Testing Sales Effect

This approach is commonly referred to as "persuasion/attitude shift". It originated in the US, where it is used to a greater extent than in the UK.

Research Method

The method is based on a "theatre test": consumers are invited to a central location, ostensibly to view a television programme (they are told this is what is being researched). One or more commercial breaks are inserted into the television programme, containing the "test" commercial along with a random selection of other commercials. Questions are asked at the start and end of the session.

The key question is asked at the start of the session, and again at the end (i.e. after exposure to the advertising). It is designed to establish consumer preference for the "test" brand. The likely effect of the advertising is judged by the "shift" in preference score for the "test" brand. (i.e. an upward shift in preference is taken to indicate a likely upward shift in sales). The attractions of this procedure are its simplicity and its claimed ability to predict a likely sales uplift (or lack thereof).

The research companies that supply this service back up their offers with case histories (in substantial numbers) designed to demonstrate their effectiveness in predicting sales uplift ("validation"). However, this approach is not without its critics, who argue that:

- the "validation" evidence is not wholly convincing (eg. little or no discussion of "failures");

- the method may have in-built biases (e.g. favours more "rational" ads, or those that contain some new item of information);

- the method assumes a "conquest" model (i.e. sales increase by bringing new consumers into the brand), whereas in practice a lot of advertising is "defensive" (designed to reinforce existing consumers).

However, arguably the biggest drawback with this approach is that it assumes a very limited role for advertising (short-term sales uplift), whereas a major preoccupation of brand owners today is with the long-term "health" of their brands, which are the guarantor of future revenues and profits.

Pre-Testing Brand Effect

This approach does not attempt to assess likely sales effect. Instead, it focuses on how the advertising is likely to effect consumer perceptions of/attachment to the brand. It is thus consistent with a more long-term view of the role of advertising in brand building and maintenance.

Research Method

The method is commonly referred to as an "impact and communication test". In practice this term covers a range of different approaches/emphases within a broadly similar framework. In a typical situation, the research is conducted in a central location, with consumers being recruited off the street. They are shown a reel of randomly selected commercials, including the "test" commercial. Questions are asked to find out if the "test" commercial was noticed, and whether the brand is recalled correctly. The "test" commercial may then be shown a second time (on its own) before more detailed questions are asked.

These questions vary (a mix of "open" and precoded questions is typically used), but may include some or all of the following:

- main content recall;
- what was perceived to be the main communication about the brand;
- questions to assess consumer "involvement" with the commercial;
- questions to assess brand image;
- questions to assess consumer "attachment" to the brand ("brand bonding").

The attractions of this approach are:

- it tries to assess the likely effect of the advertising on a broad basis (i.e. using a range of measures);
- the areas it seeks to establish measures in are those where advertising might reasonably be expected to have an effect;
- the measures are the kind of things we would want to look at in assessing "brand health".

There are two major issues/problems with this approach:

1. How do we know which measures are most important for our brand?
2. How do we interpret the "scores"?

Which Measures are Important for our Brand?

This issue is approached by considering the related questions:

- What is the nature of our brand? (Is it an essentially rational, functionally-driven brand, such as washing powder, or is it an emotionally-driven brand, such as jeans?)
- What consumer response are we trying to obtain from our advertising?

In the case of the primarily rational/functional brand, it is likely we will be seeking to communicate a tangible/rational benefit to convince consumers they should buy the brand. On the other hand, a jeans brand owner is likely to be trying to project an evocative image, which young people will want to identify with. The appropriate research measures will be different for the two brands.

The rational/functional brand will want to measure:

- Reception/understanding of the key "functional benefit" message.
- The brand image scores on the key benefit (e.g. "washes whiter").

The emotionally-driven brand will want to measure:

- Brand image scores on key emotive/evocative dimensions (e.g. "for people who are style leaders").
- Consumer "involvement" with the advertising.
- Consumer "attachment" to the brand ("brand bonding").

How do we Interpret the Scores?

This is a difficult question, and unfortunately there is no easy answer. Is a score of 40 per cent for the proportion of consumers correctly understanding our key brand benefit message good or bad? Simply put, we can't be sure. However, there are a number of ways to address the problem which should prove helpful.

1. In the case of brand image measurement, it may be possible to compare the pre-test score with a score from another data source (e.g. U&A). This should indicate whether the advertising is likely to move the brand in the desired direction. Alternatively, the pre-test can take a separate measure of image for the brand without the advertising being shown, acting as a yardstick for comparison.

2. For other pre-test scores for our brand, it may be possible to get some "feel" for their "goodness"/"badness" by comparison with scores for other brands from the research company's database. However, it is very important only to compare similar products with similar consumers.

3. It is preferable to build up one's own database of scores over time. This means one is comparing scores for the same product and the same or similar consumers.

Assessment of how the Brief is Working (or Not)

There are two objectives:

1. To check that the advertising is working the way we thought it would.
2. To provide learning/understanding that will be useful for future campaign development.

Pre-test research systems approach these tasks in two ways:

- By asking "diagnostics" questions within the regular questionnaire structure. These may be open questions, e.g. "how did you feel while watching this advertisement?", or closed questions, where consumers evaluate the advertising against a series of pre-determined dimensions e.g. "surprising", "told me something new", "made me feel good about the brand".
- By conducting small-scale qualitative research (e.g. mini groups or mini depth interviews) alongside the regular quantitative exercise.

Guidelines For Using Pre-Tests

1. Define clearly what your advertising objectives are (e.g. increase sales, reinforce existing users, contemporise the brand).
2. Define clearly how you expect the advertising to work (e.g. direct sales stimulation, communication of new information, reinforcement of brand image, change of brand image).
3. Select a pre-test system that is appropriate, and within that select appropriate measures.
4. Try to accumulate a research database over time to provide learning and perspective.

SUMMARY

Research and information for advertising development covers a lengthy sequence of procedures that progress from broad/general to highly focused/specific. It is essential to start at the beginning and work through these procedures systematically. If this is not done, the resulting advertising (and other communications) will be built on shaky foundations.

STEP 1   Review your brand in its consumer market and broader social-economic context. Use this appraisal to set realistic goals for the brand and its communications program.

STEP 2   Use early development research (before agreeing the creative brief) to better understand the current consumer context, and if necessary, to reappraise the brand positioning.

STEP 3   Use creative development research to help evaluate and optimise early creative ideas.

STEP 4   Use pre-test research to evaluate the likely effect of your finished advertising on consumer behaviour and perceptions of your brand.

Chapter 4
The Advertising Production Process

The department that looks after traffic control, production, art buying, print buying, typography and the in-house studio is known as 'creative services' and run by the creative services director. The department that produces television commercials is more simply referred to as the television department and is staffed by producers and PAs under a head of television. Growing as they do from two different disciplines, print and film, they have their own methodology.

4.1 CREATIVE SERVICES

Let's begin with creative services. Before we start the engine, we must check the oil: traffic control.

Traffic Control

Traffic's role is to monitor and inform on the agency's workflow to an agreed time and budget. Traffic has to know the exact status on any job at any given time. They are not on anyone's side. They are the unsung heroes of the advertising agency. Whether an ad is on time or on budget can mean the difference between profit and loss for even large agencies. It can lose accounts and reputations. Good agencies, like good drivers, put the best oil they can in their engines.

In many agencies, the traffic controller is also responsible for press and print production. Their role is estimating and issuing orders, buying re-touching, briefing art buying and the studio, liaising with print buyers and signing-off supplier invoices and cost controlling, all in a day's work. It's no coincidence that the traffic department is often referred to as the progress department.

Art Buyers

Put succinctly, an art buyer is responsible for sourcing photographers and illustrators, negotiating fees, issuing orders and agreeing usage.

(Creative people aren't allowed to handle money within an agency. The myth that creative people are poor businessmen still remains despite many successful agencies being run by creatives and many creative personnel being the most highly paid agency staff.)

In truth, art buyers are the eyes and ears of the art director. Creatives can't take time to keep in touch with the thousands of photographers and illustrators available. Art buyers need to have an instant response when asked: "Where can I find a car photographer?" or "Who's good with babies?"

Photographers/Illustrators

Photographers all have different areas of expertise. A car photographer will know exactly what weights to put in the boot of a plump saloon car to make it look lower and more sporty. A baby photographer will know how to keep the anxious mother relaxed, thereby not passing on their anxiety to the babies. It's only a rumour that on catalogue shoots, nappies are nailed to the floor before babies are put in them! Something that an art buyer would also be expected to know is that babies use much more film than cars.

This knowledge also has to apply to illustrators. "I've got this ad to do about a cleaner petrol – can you get me a natural history artist who understands cars? I want an engine that looks as if it's made of growing branches."

When the illustrator or photographer has delivered their product, then it's over to the print buyer. Their job is to estimate, recommend suppliers, negotiate fees, etc., but they follow the ad from finished layout to finished art, from film and cromalin through to the proof, all within the agreed time and budget.

To follow the process, first look at another flow chart on page 53 and then examine each section in more detail.

4.2 CLIENT PRESENTATION TO FINISHED EXECUTION

- The art director and art buyer begin their search for photographers or illustrators.
- A pre-estimate meeting is arranged between the account manager, the traffic controller, art buyer, the art director and the print buyer.

The Advertising Production Process

Press/Print Flowchart:
Client Presenation to Finished Execution

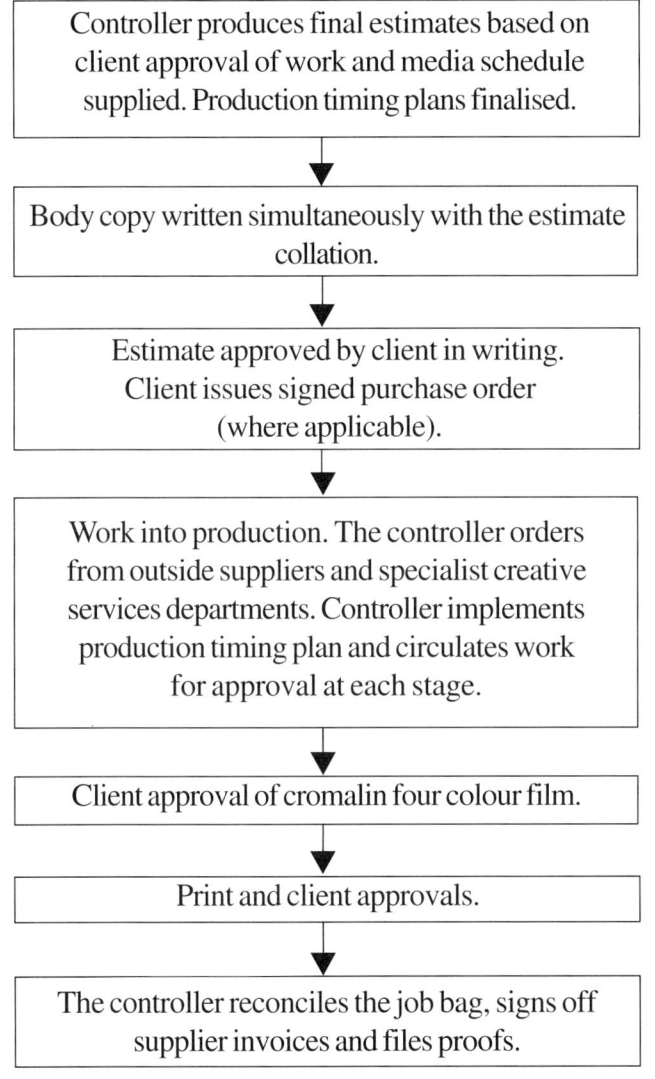

- A number of estimates need to be produced.

- The art buyer's estimate is created from information supplied by, for example, the photographer, their agent, the stylist, casting agent and model agency (for model agency also read model maker – with the advent of digital retouching, trips to the Caribbean are more likely to become trips to a model maker).

- The traffic controller is told in which media the photography/illustration will be used, for how long and where. They can then negotiate usage fees.

- The costs are collated and a production estimate prepared.

- From the schedule supplied by the media department or independent, traffic calculates the number of mechanicals, transparencies, sets of film and publication charges required.

- Estimates are then gathered from the studio for colour separations and bromides. Retouching and duplicate transparency estimates are received from an outside supplier.

- If it's print and not press, traffic now requests a print estimate, including details of packing and deliveries from the print buyer.

- A final estimate is collated and is signed by the traffic controller, head of client services, the account director and the client.

Discipline is very evident in the production process. Creatives must ensure their idea isn't modified, compromised or even lost at this stage. Approval delays can dramatically affect a job, because only when the estimate is approved by the client in writing and a signed purchase order or estimate received can money be spent on production!

Pre-Pre-Production Meeting

The first step in any production process is the pre-pre-production meeting, be it with a photographer or illustrator. To ensure the job is on brief and to schedule, the art buyer arranges for the outside supplier (the photographer or illustrator) to meet the creative team and the traffic controller. The brief is discussed: props, locations, models – everything of significance is considered.

Pre-Production Meeting

The next meeting involves the client and requires their approval to recommendations made by the photographer, illustrator and art director. At this stage, the responsibility is handed back to the creative team. What might have been anything from a one-stroke scribble to a highly finished layout is about to become an ad.

Clients rarely attend stills shoots. They are a slow, meticulous, repetitious activity with little opportunity for input from those not involved. Of the many images taken, the photographer will make their selection from the point of view of photographic quality. The art director will then make their choice, considering impact, clarity, relevance, etc. The creative director endorses his recommendation. Only then will the rest of the team pass comment and the transparency be passed on for client approval.

Meanwhile, the copywriter will have received approval of the body copy.

Armed with the approved layout, copy transparency/illustration and media, traffic briefs the typographer, who begins work on the master mechanical (the coming together of all of the above elements as a flat artwork). Art director and typographer confer. A typeface and style is agreed on.

The transparency or illustration is scanned into the typographer's computer, and in the case of a transparency, released to an outside supplier for re-touching. There is a rigorous signing-off stage before the master mechanical can be adapted for different media sizes. These days, most mechanicals are held and created on disk.

Next comes the four colour separations. Printed colour images are made up of a red, yellow, blue and black plates. It is the outside reprohouse who does this work, supplying a cromalin to the agency. The production head and the art director suggest any colour corrections and the final proof is signed-off by the creative director.

It is at this stage that the client becomes involved again. Their approval signature is required to release material to the publications or for bulk printing. Once the job has been despatched, traffic checks all the costs against the supplier invoices, reconciles the job bag and files the proof, either into a guard book or onto CD-ROM.

The art director goes home to their mum and shows her the ad in the magazine. The conversation goes something like this:

"Look Mum. My ad."
"That's nice dear. Did you take that lovely photograph?"
"No."
"What about the words – are they yours?"
"No, I work with a writer."
"So you did the layout?"
"No, that was done in the studio."
"You chose the typeface?"
"No, that's the typographer's job."
"Are you sure it's your ad dear?"
"Yes Mum, it was my idea."
"Idea? Oh, I see dear."

Ideas can easily get lost in this process and the art director deserves a lot of credit just for protecting the idea, let alone improving it during production. Even so, this is a much more satisfactory conversation than the copywriter can have when they take their commercial home, or indeed the client who proudly declares, "Did you see my ad?" to anyone who'll listen.

Advertising Agency Producer

When we look at television and radio production, both the traffic controller and the art buyer merge into one – the advertising agency producer. Theirs is a highly complicated multi-disciplined role, involving the worlds of creativity, finance, IT and time management.

The agency producer's first task is to help the creative team select an outside film production company. There are thousands of these, consisting of anything from a director and producer team in one room up to major operations employing 30 or 40 people running their own studios.

Producers and Directors

How do they choose? A producer's main requirement is a thorough knowledge of the market. Every director has a showreel. Producers watch them constantly, whether for a specific job or not.

Directors tend to specialise (they would insist they are pigeon-holed). A table-top director may have stills background and use their meticulous eye for detail to produce exquisite still lifes. This specialisation may break down even further if the director is a food expert. There are even directors who specialise solely in chocolate. None of these are likely to be asked to do a fast-action, location shoot. Others specialise in dialogue or personality presenter commercials, often coming from a television background.

Directors can come from the agency creative side. This can be a bonus because they understand the commercial side of film-making. Others take the pop-promo route to advertising. It's even been known for a director to come up through film school!

Features directors pick up commercials between cinema projects, often using revenue from advertising to fund their first career choice. This can cause problems for agency producers dealing with a campaign. "I'm sorry, he's off on a feature for six months" are words best avoided when you've got an air date twelve weeks away.

Nevertheless, directors do attach themselves to campaigns. Tony Smith directed Maureen Lipman in the BT ads for many years, moving on to direct Pauline Quirke and Linda Robson (*Birds of a Feather*) for Surf. Derek Coutts not only directed the Nescafé couples in the UK, Nestlé went on to use his skills all around the world as it became a global campaign.

Finding the right person is only one aspect of the producer's job. Finding them at the right prices is also essential. Budgets are always tight, whether they are £50,000 or £500,000. Clients and agencies will both want to squeeze every ounce of value out of them.

Some major clients employ independent cost controllers to vet an agency's quotation, demonstrating how complex this area is. The skill is to find directors on their way up or down who are producing work better than their price suggests and then negotiate hard.

If there are ten scenes in a 30 second commercial quoted at £200,000, it doesn't mean they are all three seconds long and cost £20,000 each. Producers have to be able to look at a script and know what's expensive about it. Is the most expensive scene the most important? How important is it that we use a helicopter shot to pull back from the skiers to see the client's logo etched in the snow? Could we use a crane or even a model-maker? Surely we can do it in post-production on Henry, Flame or whatever the latest state of the art digital technology is most appropriate.

More and more, post-production is being handled by the agency, not the outside production company. It's an expensive business renting a digital suite at several hundred pounds an hour. The agency might as well put its mark-up on it, rather than mark-up an already marked-up production company estimate. Yet it's as much about control as cost and once more, it's the producer who has the responsibility. Keeping up to date with the latest digital technology advances would be a job in itself in any other industry.

The final and most crucial skill required of producers is time management. Like budgets, deadlines are always tight. Client research will have to be accommodated, artists' and directors' availability assessed, time for suitable locations to be found, models need to be made, etc. No client likes paying late copy playout charges. No client stays with an agency that misses an airdate.

If the agency producer's job seems at all stressful, it's because it is. They are responsible for both the agency's and client's financial success. Even so, few clients get close to agency producers in the way they get close to creative people or account handlers. Perhaps they should.

The production now enters a crucial stage for client and agency alike, a phase when they both check to see if they're speaking the same language, or indeed making the same film.

Pre-Production and Final Pre-Production Meetings

Two meetings take place chaired by the agency producer, the pre-production meeting and the final pre-production meeting. Attendees are the same on both occasions: the director and production company producer, the creative team, the account management team and the client. Timing of these meetings in relation to the shoot date should be predetermined by the agency producer. The first meeting should give sufficient preparation time, but also take place early enough for agreed changes to be put in place in time for the second meeting.

The final pre-production meeting is best used as a final check and 'signing-off' session rather than a decision-making occasion. It begins with a restatement of the objectives of the campaign provided by the account management team. This may appear repetitious but in fact it could be the first time the film has been discussed this way in front of the director.

The script and its necessary legal and technical clearances are examined. By now a script will have gone through many drafts and the most recent additions or alterations are likely to be for legal rather than commercial reasons, so it is essential to agree that this is the final script.

Casting is covered, with the main characters being shown to the client on video for final approval. Directors and agency creatives attend casting sessions where 30 or 40 people are seen for each part. It is their selection which is shown to the client. Wardrobe is discussed, location photographers or set designs are produced, and key props are displayed.

It is around now that the meeting often gets bogged down in the colour of a particular towel or the style of a handbag. Agency and client must stay focused on the key issues. This is not about personal preference. The consumer should be the final style guru.

Products and packs are discussed. Designs may have been simplified for the camera. Technical people may be requested to attend the shoot to ensure the 'liquid' is the correct thickness and colour. Music is aired, either a library track or composer's demo. Using a director's storyboard (as opposed to the agency board) the client is taken through the shoot, scene by scene. Key frame objectives are required by some clients.

Yet most importantly the director takes everyone through their interpretation of the script. Remember, this is often the only time a director and client meet. It is essential to make a good impression.

The agency producer will have had this in mind when choosing a director, asking themselves questions, such as "Can this young pop promo find be put in front of my client after a night on the town and still wearing a nose ring?" or "Is an established director with 30 years experience right for this innovative, youth-orientated client?"

The meeting concludes with the relevant insurance covers and production schedules.

Minutes of the meeting are produced by the agency producer's PA and issued within 24 hours to all attendees. The client should now know what to expect and the agency know what to shoot.

Filming

As national brands become international and international brands become global, these two meetings become more and more significant. Just taking one item on the agenda, casting, we can see the complexity of choosing an actress who can play a housewife in the UK, Greece, Beunos Aries and Scandinavia. (She is likely to be a blonde because Greeks and Argentinians find blondes up market.) As for the colour and style of handbag, the possibilities are endless.

Like stills, clients rarely attend film shoots more than once. If they do, they will likely comment on the number of people standing around doing nothing. Film-making is a technical, highly professional activity. It is very difficult for an outsider to understand the complexity of what's happening.

Many clients sensibly leave it to the agency, not only because it is best to let them get on with it unhindered, but also because if the agency has total responsibility, the client can retain their objectivity rather than be involved in any buck passing after the event. The person with ultimate responsibility on the day of filming is the director. Traditionally, any comments from the agency creative team are passed on to the agency producer, then to the production company producer and so to the director. However, all shades of relationships exist.

Filming is viewed on an instant video link offering playback of each take, even a rough assembly of an edit, making the agency much more aware of what it is getting. This is a stark contrast to the old days (less than ten years ago) when you had to wait for the following day's rushes before being able to make a judgement.

After filming is completed, the agency producer ensures they have all the artists' invoices. The crew and studio costs are paid by the production company.

A voiceover and studio time is booked, and the director produces their cut with the editor. The creative team approves the cut and attends the recording and dubbing of soundtrack sessions.

Prior to showing a client the cut, the agency has its own internal approval procedure. The account team pass their comments only after the film has been seen and approved by the creative director. As the one person involved in every aspect of the commercial, it is essential for the agency producer to be present at the client presentation. A preamble to the presentation will explain that the film hasn't been graded, the quality is only that of a low resolution Avid Edit, the dub is only rough, the voice a guide track, etc.

The client might wonder what they are approving. The alternative, however, is to needlessly spend money that has to be re-spent if the edit is not approved unchanged. Next, the final voiceover is recorded, the film is graded to the correct light and colour balance and the titles are added.

Questions and changes at this stage can prove expensive and the producer needs to be on hand to either accept financial responsibility or explain to the client why it should be at their expense.

Post-Production Stage

It is unusual nowadays for films not to have a post-production stage. As previously stated, the agency takes financial responsibility for this rather than the production company. The director might charge for their time, particularly if they had been hired in the first place for their technical expertise.

Image distortion, morphing and other digital effects (especially computer-generated sequences) require expensive people and equipment. The agency producer needs to be aware of the very latest technology.

Before the film can go on the air, a final post-production script and film have to be sent to the BACC (or country equivalent) to check that the film obeys all the voluntary codes laid down by the industry.

The television administration department pays the production company its second 50 per cent. The artists' repeat fees are passed for payment. Music copyright data is passed to the Performing Rights Society, and a finished film is put on file in the archive library.

The agency producer staggers home to mum. Over the weekend the ad is on. The conversation goes something like this.

 Mum: *"Is this your ad dear?"*
 Producer: *"Yes."*
 Mum: *"What did you do?"*
 Producer: *(collapsing into chair) "Everything!"*

Creative Development (from Creative Brief to Client Presentation)	
New television campaign	6 weeks
New television ad in existing campaign	4 weeks
New press/poster/radio campaign	4 weeks
New press/poster/radio ad in existing campaign	3 weeks
Brochures	8 weeks
Direct mail/sales promotion	4 weeks
Internet	8 weeks
CD-ROM	8 weeks

Traffic Flowchart System to Client Presentation

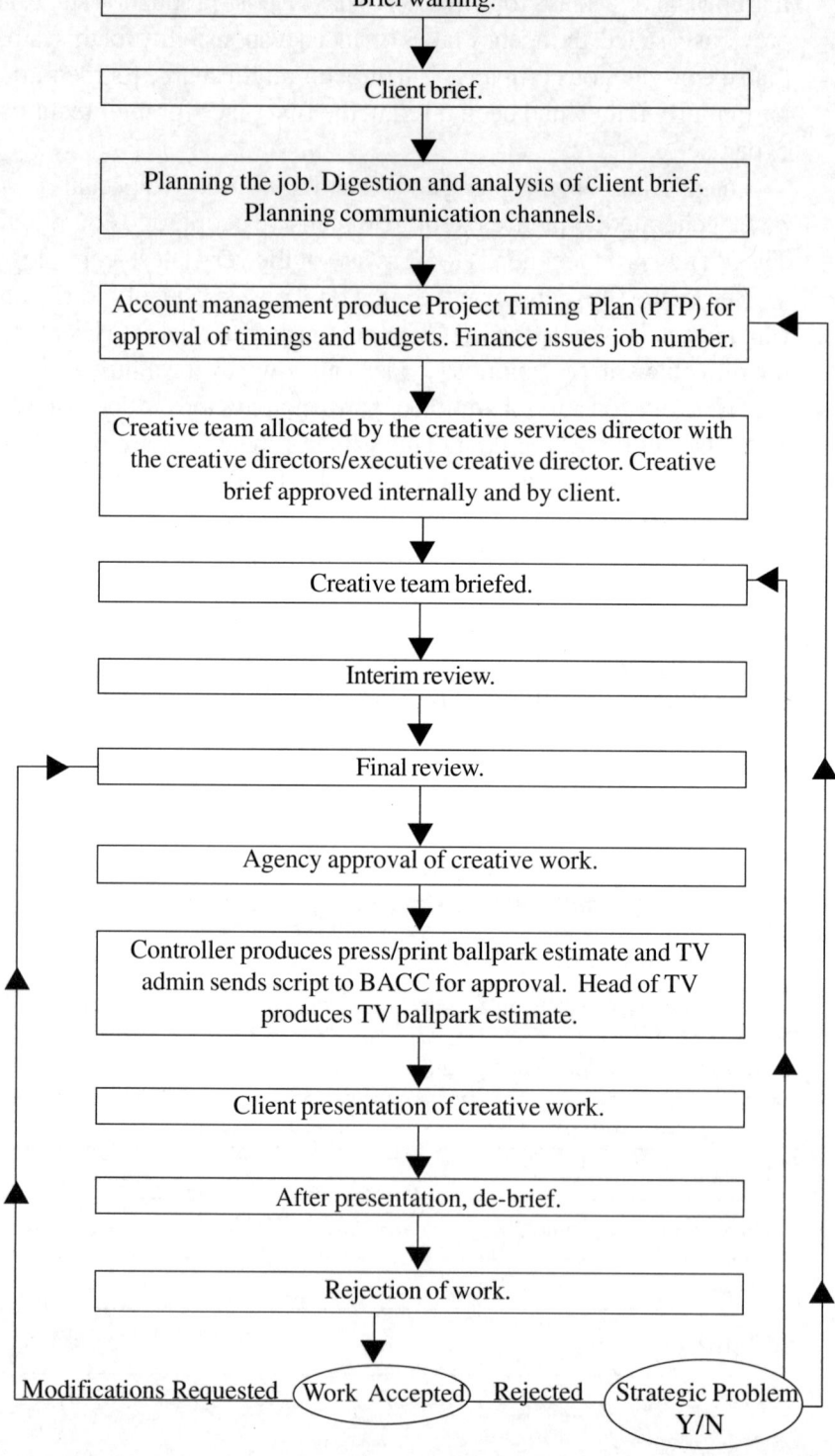

Chapter 5
Asessing the Effects of Advertising

The effects of advertising are generally felt among a range of audiences, most obviously consumers, but also retailers/distributors, sales people, company employees, etc. For the purposes of this chapter, the focus will be exclusively on the main role of advertising – its effect on the consumer.

How advertising works is a notoriously difficult area and is the subject of considerable industry/academic debate. The view taken here is that advertising has two primary objectives:

1. To sustain/develop brands as entities that exist in consumer's minds.
2. To influence consumer behaviour in respect of any given brand.

These two objectives are interrelated.

5.1 SUSTAINING/DEVELOPING BRANDS

It is difficult to disagree with the idea that brands are very important, and becoming even more so:

- They are what consumers buy and use to obtain satisfactions over and above those provided by the products themselves (consider the satisfactions delivered by a BMW compared to those delivered by a similarly specified Ford).
- Brands are increasingly recognised (by accountants as well as marketing people) as prime corporate assets, the key instruments to deliver ongoing revenues and profit margins.

Advertising, a controllable, flexible and intrusive form of marketing communication, is generally accepted as a powerful tool for brand sustenance and development.

5.2 INFLUENCING CONSUMER BEHAVIOUR

Advertising can influence consumer behaviour in a number of ways, most prominently by:

- reminding/reinforcing ongoing purchasing of an established brand;
- acting to stimulate increased purchasing by recruiting new users, or by increasing weight of usage among existing consumers (for example, by suggesting new uses).

There is a close relationship between sustaining brands and influencing behaviour.

Generally, advertising should act in both 'brand sustenance' and 'behaviour influencing' mode – the two objectives are usually complementary. Thus, in the reinforcement situation, repeat purchasing (behaviour) is reinforced by reminding the consumer of the brand's core benefits (brand sustenance).

5.3 BRANDS

If brands are the central focus of advertising activity, it is essential to understand how brands work. Put simply, a typical brand works as follows.

1. It is designed to appeal to a specific group of consumers ('target market') whose needs are clearly understood.

2. The brand offer is constructed to satisfy those needs, both functional (i.e. product performance) and emotional (e.g. prestige).

3. The fit between target market needs and brand offer (functional/emotional) is known as the brand positioning.

4. Over time, the brand also develops additional values and associations that are consistent with and serve to reinforce the core brand positioning.

Brand Model

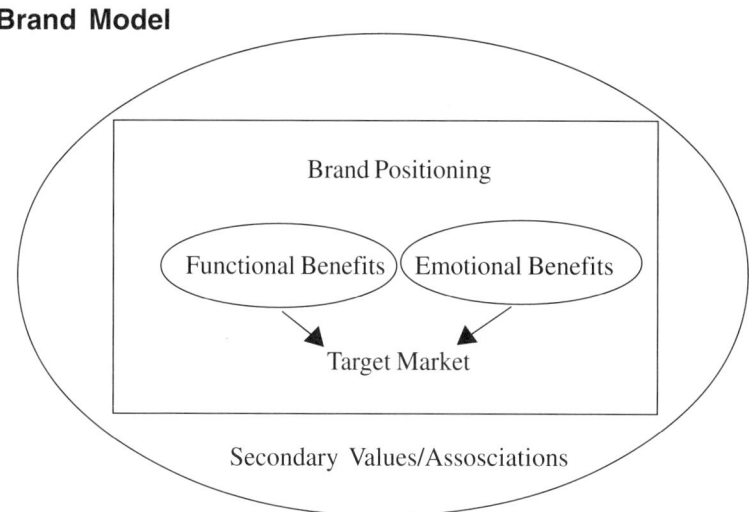

Brands operate along the spectrum between functional and emotional benefits. An example from each end of the spectrum could be:

100% functional brand = 'permanently low price'.
100% emotional brand = fragrance brand appealing purely on its image.

In practice, most brands offer a combination of functional and emotional benefits, though the emphasis on each will vary.

Implications for Advertising

Arguably, the single most important task for advertising is to communicate the brand positioning to the target market. Initially, this can be done by establishing the positioning, and, subsequently, by reminding/reinforcing.

In a crowded/competitive market, the advertising is saying, "You (group of consumers) – this brand has been created specifically to meet your needs, and will do so better than any other brand." Some communication of the brand positioning, even if only in abbreviated/reminder form, should be built into all advertising.

Communicating the Brand Positioning

How the advertising attempts to communicate the positioning will be affected by the nature of the positioning.

- *Functional positionings,* which are based on product and/or price benefits, are intrinsically rational and are expressed via 'persuasion' advertising. Such advertising seeks to persuade the consumer by communicating the rational product benefit (e.g. 'washes whiter').
- *Emotional positionings* are by their nature non-rational: they work via processes such as identification ('this brand is just right for my lifestyle') or empathy (the generation of 'warm feelings' towards the brand).

Advertising that communicates in this way is known as involvement advertising, i.e. it involves the consumer emotionally. Given that most brands combine functional and emotional elements, it is logical that most advertising tends to do the same (albeit with varying emphasis).

Basic Role/Objectives of Advertising

To summarise, briefly, where we are now:

- Advertising seeks to do two things:
  - sustain a brand and its consumer appeal;
  - influence consumer behaviour in respect of the brand.
- The two objectives are interrelated. Advertising that is effective should generally achieve both effects (even if the behavioural effect is simple reinforcement).
- Within brand sustenance, effective, ongoing communication of the brand positioning is the primary objective.
- The nature of the brand positioning (e.g. emphasis on functional or emotional elements) will affect the style of advertising (persuasion or involvement).

Brand Situation

Unfortunately, this essentially simple way of thinking about advertising objectives and effects is complicated by the situation the brand is in. If we exclude new brands and new products (which form a special subject in their own right), we can distinguish three main types of brand situations as follows.

Brand Situation	Marketing Objectives	Role of Advertising	
		Brand	Behaviour
Maintenance	Maintain existing consumers and purchasing (maintain SOM)	Reinforce/ remind	Reinforce/ remind
Growth	a) new penetration b) increased weight of use (increase SOM)	Limited change (no change to brand positioning)	Change
Reinvention	New brand positioning	Radical	Change

SOM = Share of Market

This brand situation framework indicates the broad thrust of a brand's likely objectives and the implications for the role of advertising.

At the detail level of individual brands, the specifics of the situation will vary. For example:

- Brand A is pursuing a new penetration strategy, designed to extend the brand into a younger (under 30) age group. This requires new advertising designed to freshen and rejuvenate the brand (without changing the core brand positioning).

- Brand B is pursuing an increased weight of use strategy, designed to increase the brand's share of repertoire purchasing. This necessitates a simple upweight of existing advertising, targeted against heavy repertoire consumers.

Maintenance is about more than just reiterating the brand positioning. It might also include:

- communication of a product improvement to maintain the functional adequacy of the brand.
- A new campaign to freshen the brand and maintain contemporarneity.

5.4 SETTING SPECIFIC ADVERTISING OBJECTIVES

We are now in a position to set out our specific advertising objectives and the resulting effects we are looking to achieve:

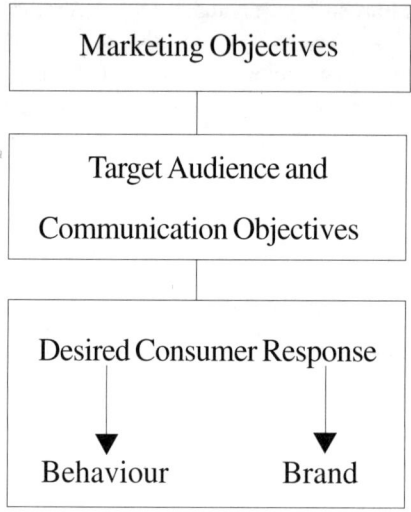

For example, a 'New World' wine brand has been available for a number of years, and has slowly built volume on the basis of good product quality and distinctive taste. The current consumer base is mainly connoisseurs/wine afficianiados. Advertising support has been limited to up-market press.

The brand owner wishes to grow volume more rapidly by extending appeal to a broader market – more experimental/open-minded, ordinary (non-connoisseur) wine drinkers. This will entail a heavier weight of advertising, using a broader range of media. As part of this process he wants to build emotional values into the brand to enhance brand appeal to the more ordinary drinker. The chosen core emotional value is 'open-mindedness', reflecting both the brand's New World provenance and its rather distinctive taste.

Marketing Objective	Extend penetration.
Target Audience	More experimental, ordinary wine drinkers.
Communication Objectives	1. Raise brand salience. 2. Communicate the brand's core functional and emotional benefits (distinctive taste/open-minded persona). 3. Stimulate trial.
Desired Consumer Response: **Behaviour**	Brand trial. Heightened awareness. Registration of the core functional benefit (distinctive taste). Identification with the brand's 'open-mindedness'.

5.5 THE EVALUATION OF ADVERTISING EFFECTS

Once the desired advertising effects (or consumer responses) have been precisely defined, the evaluation process is, in principle, straightforward (although frequently tricky at the detail level). This involves:

- setting up appropriate measurement processes (behaviour/brand);
- measuring what effects are achieved;
- as far as possible, trying to eliminate the effects of other major marketing activity (your own and your competitors') to leave a residual advertising effect.

Formal evaluation uses these measures to answer the question: "How far have we achieved/failed to achieve our objectives?" Where the answer is 'failure', it seeks to answer the question: 'why?'

5.6 EVALUATION OF ADVERTISING EFFECTS ON CONSUMER BEHAVIOUR

By 'consumer behaviour' we mean two things:
1. Consumer purchasing of our brand.
2. Consumer usage of our brand.

There are a number of research tools available for measurement of purchasing and usage:

Purchasing	Usage
Consumer panels.	Consumer panels.
Retail audits.	Consumer surveys.
Ex-factory deliveries.	
Consumer surveys.	
Industry sales data.	

The different research tools have different strengths/weaknesses:

PURCHASING		
Research Tool	Strengths	Weaknesses
Consumer Panel	Direct consumer purchasing data.	Less accurate than retail audits.
Retail Audit	Accurate, rapid sales measure (and price, distribution).	Sales, price, distribution data only – not consumer data.
Ex-factory Deliveries	Approximate sales measure.	No consumer data.
Consumer Surveys	Clamed consumer purchasing.	Typically not very accurate.

USAGE		
Consumer Panel	Direct consumer usage data.	Panel size may limit accuracy.
Consumer Survey	Claimed usage.	Typically less accurate than panel.

For examination of consumer purchasing, the two most useful research tools are the *consumer panel* and the *retail audit*.

The *consumer panel* provides measures of:

- consumer purchases (i.e. sales);
- price;
- whether or not the product was bought on promotion.

In addition, it allows us to examine consumer behaviour measures for the total population and discrete sub-groups (e.g. demographic groups, our brand buyers, heavy buyers). These measures include:

- penetration;
- weight of purchase;
- repeat purchase;
- share of repertoire;
- gains/loss against competitors.

Consumer panels are therefore a very useful tool for examination of the direct behavioural effect of advertising.

The *retail audit*, in its modern EPOS guise, provides speed and accuracy in the measurement of sales, price and whether the product was bought on promotion. The major limitations of the retail audit are:

- The coverage of the audit. (Does it measure all the relevant retail outlets?)
- Lack of information at the consumer level (e.g. penetration, etc.).

Both consumer panels and retail audits can be used for econometric modelling, a powerful tool with which to unravel the effects of advertising from other marketing activity (such as price/promotions).

For examination of *consumer usage* of a brand, both consumer panels and consumer surveys have their weaknesses (typically lack of absolute accuracy), but are generally adequate to register a clear change in usage (e.g. a new usage mode). Note that the consumer panels used to measure usage are different from those used to measure purchasing.

Direct Evaluation of Consumer Behaviour

The simplest way to examine the behavioural effect of advertising is by looking for change (or stability) directly at the consumer level. The examples below indicate the types of behaviour change (or stability) one would be looking for. Consumer panels are the best source of this kind of data.

Maintenance	Continuation of a steady pattern of 'repeat buying' for our brand.
Growth a) *new penetration*	Increased penetration of our brand among the designated new target market.
b) *increased weight of use*	An increase in our brand's 'share of repertoire' or our brand being used in a new way.
Reinvention (new positioning)	Increasing penetration of our brand among its new target market (and new method of usage).

Indirect Evaluation of Consumer Behaviour

In the absence of reliable direct measures of consumer behaviour, consumer sales (the ultimate objective of all marketing activity, including advertising) can be used as an indirect measure.

In this situation, the appropriate measures would be:

Maintenance	Steady ongoing sales/SOM.
New penetration/ increased weight of use	Sales/SOM increase.
Reinvention (new positioning)	Sales/SOM increase (assuming that the new positioning has greater consumer appeal than the discarded one).

SOM (share of market) is generally a better measure than simple consumer sales – it eliminates the effects of external factors (e.g. hot summer) that may distort the market, and hence our brand's sales.

Evaluating Advertising Effects versus Other Effects on Consumer Behaviour

Thus far we have evaluated the effect of advertising simply by looking for change (or stability) in consumer behaviour (purchasing/usage). We have not taken account of other marketing activity – our own or competitors' – which may also impact consumer behaviour. The most important types of marketing activity for consideration are generally:

Distribution change	(us/competition)
Price change	(us/competition)
Major promotion	(us/competition)
Competitor advertising	

There are three ways we can address this issue, in ascending order of complexity:

1. observation;
2. area test;
3. econometrics.

1. Observation

This is the simplest approach, where we look at all the available evidence on the effects of different types of marketing activity on our brand and try to apply the information in a common sense way.

For example, historical experience might indicate the following typical effects:

MARKETING ACTIVITY	EFFECT ON OUR BRAND
Our brand increases distribution by 10%	+1-3% SOM
Price promotion for our brand	+5-10% SOM (during promotion)
Major competitor price promotion	-3-5% SOM (during promotion)

If, during the period our advertising is running, our brand increases distribution by 5 per cent, a competitor runs a price promotion, and during this period our brand SOM increases by 5 per cent, we might conclude that this was a fairly robust advertising effect.

2. Area Test

Area testing is a somewhat more rigorous way of trying to isolate the effects of advertising on our brand. The procedure is to leave one or two 'areas' (e.g. television regions) unadvertised, then observe the difference in brand performance (direct consumer behaviour measures and/or consumer sales) between advertised and unadvertised areas. In principle, this gives a clear measure of the effect of the advertising. However, for this measurement to be valid, all other possible influencing factors should be (more or less) equal across advertised and unadvertised areas.

Influencing factors include area characteristics – population profile, retail profile, etc. – and market/brand specific factors, such as usage of the product category, brand distribution and brand share. Perfect or near perfect symmetry between advertised and non-advertised areas is rarely achieved. Additionally, competitors can deliberately spoil a test area by running a deep price promotion or other such measures.

In spite of these drawbacks, area tests can often provide a reasonably good indication, if not a precise measure, of the nature/direction of advertising effects.

3. Econometrics

Econometrics (or econometric modelling) is the name given to a statistical procedure that tries to model the effects of different types of marketing activity on brand performance (consumer sales/SOM). As such, it essentially does the same thing as the common sense observation approach, but in a more rigorous and precise way. The key material required for successful modelling is a reasonably long sequence (e.g. 2-3 years) of measures of brand SOM and key marketing activity – advertising, distribution, pricing, promotions, etc.

The data is computer analysed, using a technique called multiple regression, to produce an estimate of the magnitude of effect any given marketing activity typically has on our brand.

For example, the analysis might indicate that changes in our brand's SOM are accounted for primarily by price (40 per cent), secondly by advertising (20 per cent) and thirdly by distribution (15 per cent).

The major advantages of econometric modelling are:

- it measures the relative sensitivity of our brand to different marketing activity;
- it allows one to simulate different market scenarios, e.g. where we might double advertising expenditures, or halve advertising expenditures in combination with a price cut.

These are two major caveats with regard to econometric modelling:

1. It is neither perfect nor totally scientific – the modeller's skill and experience typically play some part in the model.
2. It only explains short-term variations in a brand's SOM, not the underlying SOM that tends to remain relatively stable in the long-term (and is arguably driven by the brand's consumer pull).

5.7 EVALUATION OF BRAND EFFECTS ON ADVERTISING

The effects of advertising on the brand are best examined in two ways:
1. Direct effects on the brand.
2. Advertising/consumer interaction.

Direct effects on the brand looks at the direct effects of advertising on the consumer's perception of and feelings about the brand.

Advertising/consumer interaction looks at how the advertising impacts on and communicates with the consumer and how the consumer responds to the advertising. This provides an indication of the way(s) the advertising is likely to effect the brand, and is particularly useful where the direct effects on the brand may take some time to become apparent.

5.8 DIRECT EFFECTS ON THE BRAND

There are three main areas for consideration:
1. Brand salience.
2. Consumer perceptions of the brand.
3. Consumer feelings towards the brand.

Brand Salience

By 'brand salience' we mean two things:
- Is the consumer aware of the brand?
- How 'top of mind' is the brand?

Brand salience is important for two reasons:
1. As a basic indicator of brand presence in its market (or market segment for a 'niche' brand).
2. In certain types of market (e.g. fragmented markets, repertoire markets, impulse markets), brand salience can be an important determinant of consumer propensity to purchase.

There are two basic measures of brand salience – *unprompted awareness* and *prompted awareness*. *Unprompted awareness* asks what brands a consumer can think of in a given market, and the answers may be recorded in sequence (first mention, second mention, etc.). *Prompted awareness* asks the same question, but consumers are shown a list of the main brands to help them.

Typically, prompted brand awareness increases as a result of advertising more readily than unprompted awareness. However, unprompted awareness is the more important measure for brand advantage in fragmented, repertoire and impulse markets.

Consumer Perceptions of the Brand

Under this heading, we are interested in the answer to the question: "How does the consumer perceive our brand?"

More specifically, we are interested in knowing what they think about:

- what it is;
- what is does/who it is for;
- what benefits it offers;
- what features/attributes it has;
- what values it is associated with;
- what its personality is like;
- how it is different from competitors'.

Consumer perceptions of our brand and competitor brands are typically measured using a brand image question format. The interviewer works through a sequence of statements (e.g. 'a brand that really gets stains out', 'a brand for young people') and consumers indicate which brands they apply to. A carefully constructed question sequence should be able to profile the emotional (non-functional) and functional aspects of a brand. This produces a profile of each brand, showing its overall characteristics and particular strengths and weaknesses against the competition.

There are two important things to bear in mind when measuring consumer perceptions via brand image questions.

First, before you construct your list of statements for the question sequence, draw up a subjective brand profile for your brand and key

competitor brands. The brand profile should specify:
- key functional benefit(s);
- key emotional benefit(s);
- key attributes/features;
- key values;
- key personality elements;
- target consumers;
- target usage occasions.

Your question sequence should contain statements designed to measure consumer perceptions of the most important items in the brand profile. As an example, let's look at a speciality yoghurt from Japan that helps maintain stomach acid balance.

BRAND PROFILE	
Functional benefit(s)	Maintains a healthy stomach (and hence healthy digestion).
Emotional benefit(s)	Healthy, vibrant outlook on life.
Attributes/Features	Mild taste and creamy texture.
Values	Healthy, natural, authentic, pure.
Personality	Outgoing, youthful, vibrant, optimistic.
Target Consumers	Young women.
Target Occasions	Lunch, mid-morning snack, mid-afternoon snack.

Sample statements for the question sequence:
- Keeps your digestion in top condition.
- Keeps you feeling vibrant.
- Delicious creamy taste.
- For outgoing people.
- Suitable for lunch.
- A natural way to stay healthy.
- For people with a positive outlook.

Secondly, when interpreting results of the question sequence, take the effect of brand size into account. Large brands typically obtain high scores for most statements in brand image questions because more consumers are familiar with them. Small brands typically obtain much lower scores.

Therefore, it is important to remove the brand size effect from the data in order to obtain a clear reading of the relative strengths/weaknesses of the different brands. This is done by means of a mathematical technique know as 'deviations from expected', which can be applied by the research supplier.

Consumer Feelings towards the Brand

There are three further areas for examination under this heading:

a) The consumer/brand relationship.

b) Consumer/brand attachment.

c) The value a consumer places on the brand.

The Consumer/Brand Relationship

Consumers can relate to brands in a number of ways. Some of the most prominent consumer/brand relationships include:

1. Functional (uses this brand because it does the job).

2. Authority (uses this brand because they know it's the best).

3. Helper (uses this brand because it helps to keep the kids quiet).

4. Identification (wears this brand because it's a brand for 'cool' people).

The brand/consumer relationship is important because it defines the brand's role in the consumer's life and helps to reinforce ongoing brand usage.

A reasonable indication of the nature and strength of the consumer/brand relationship can generally be obtained by use of one or more appropriate statements in a brand image question. Alternatively, the relationship can be more fully explored in qualitative research.

Consumer/Brand Attachment

The single most important objective of branding is to build consumer attachment (or loyalty) to the brand. The nature of consumer attachment to a brand will vary. More functional brands tend to build attachment on a (rational) belief in the efficacy of their product performance whereas more emotional brands generally seek to build attachment via some form of involvement.

Consumer/brand attachment is measured via loyalty ladders. These use a sequence of questions to sort consumers into a hierarchy of attachment to the brand. Those at the top of the hierarchy who are most strongly attached to the brand might be classified as 'loyal' or 'bonded'. Those in the middle may be classified as 'semi-committed', while those towards the bottom of the hierarchy may be either indifferent to the brand or even hostile.

Loyalty ladders come in different guises and from different origins or theoretical starting points. It is worth considering how well a loyalty ladder fits the circumstances of your brand before using it.

The Value a Consumer Places on the Brand

The ultimate value of a brand lies not just in its ability to generate loyalty (and hence repeat buying), but also its ability to command a worthwhile price (profitable margin for the brand owner).

There are three ways to assess the consumer value of a brand:

- Blind/branded product test.
- Brand/price trade-off.
- Brand/price demand curve.

Blind/branded product test

The research process for the blind/branded product test involves getting a sample of consumers to use the product and evaluate its performance, first in 'blind' (i.e. unbranded) mode, and then in branded mode.

The blind and branded products are both rated on key performance dimensions and also on some 'softer' dimensions (e.g. suitability for different types of people or different occasions). A purchase interest question is asked, e.g. "How likely are you to buy this product/brand?"

The difference in scores between the blind and branded evaluations indicates the extent to which the brand is adding value to the basic product in terms of enhanced purchase interest, better performance scores or better scores for 'softer' (non-performance) measures. In effect, this gives us a non-price measure of the consumer value of the brand.

Brand/price trade-off

This is a research procedure that assesses the extent to which consumers will continue to buy a brand as its price is progressively increased. The end result is a price curve that demonstrates how purchase interest in the brand declines as the price rises. This gives us a price-based measure of the consumer value of the brand.

Brand/price demand curve

This provides the same kind of information as the brand/price trade-off, but does so by plotting actual (real world) brand SOM at different price levels. A brand/price demand curve can only be generated if consumer purchasing (consumer panel) or consumer sales (retail audit) data are available.

5.9 EVALUATING THE DIRECT EFFECTS OF ADVERTISING ON THE BRAND: SHORT-TERM VERSUS LONG-TERM

It is generally best to separate medium/long-term objectives for the brand from more immediate/short-term objectives. For example, a medium-term objective might be to enhance consumer perceptions of brand quality, whereas the short-term objective might be to communicate a product quality upgrade as the first step in the quality enhancement process.

Medium/long-term brand status (i.e. brand health) is best measured at reasonably spaced intervals (yearly or less frequently), using a U&A type of research vehicle. This allows a lengthy questionnaire with which to measure/assess all the important elements of the brand. Brand attachment and brand value measures should also form part of the medium-term health check. The medium/long-term advertising effect is then judged by the extent to which the brand is on course against its predetermined objectives within the maintenance/growth/reinvention framework.

Short-term brand effects tend to be more immediately important in the brand growth or brand reinvention situations. Here we will be looking for the advertising to create change in brand salience and/or consumer feelings and perceptions of the brand. In this case, measurement of the advertising effects needs to be made immediately following the advertising. A continuous tracking study or pre/post approach (e.g. using an omnibus survey) is the most appropriate research vehicle. The short-term advertising effect is judged by the extent to which relevant brand measures change after the advertising.

5.10 CONSUMER/ADVERTISING INTERACTION

Here we are interested in:

- The extent to which the advertising has been *noticed* by the consumer.
- What the advertising seems to be *communicating* to the consumer.
- How the consumer seems to be *responding* to the advertising.

The reason for being interested in these things is that they are indicators of whether or not the advertising is likely to achieve its planned effects on the brand.

Noticeability of the advertising is the most questionable indicator: there is some evidence that noticeability of advertising is associated with sales increases, but on the other hand, there is evidence of advertising that has achieved good brand or sales effects without being strongly noticed.

Advertising *communication* is a clear indicator: if the advertising is not communicating as intended, it is unlikely that the desired effects will feed through to the brand.

Consumer *response* is also important: if consumers respond negatively to a piece of advertising, it becomes less likely that they will receive the intended communication.

- **Noticeability**. Advertising noticeability is typically measured by a question that asks 'what brand of......(category) have you seen advertised recently?' The question may be asked unprompted or prompted (i.e. showing a list of relevant brands to aid recall). This produces a measure known as advertising awareness, or advertising recall.

- **Communication**. Advertising communication is typically assessed by a question along the lines of 'what was the advertising trying to tell you?' The difficulty is that questions such as this may work less well for involvement advertising that isn't trying to tell you something as much as draw you into an emotionally based game. In such cases, it may be necessary to use qualitative research to draw out the full communication to the consumer.

- **Consumer Response**. By 'consumer response' we mean:
    - What does the consumer think about this piece of advertising?
    - How does he/she feel about it (positive/negative/indifferent)?

    Structured questions are typically used to assess response: the consumer is read a sequence of words/phrases ('entertaining', 'lively', 'boring', etc.) and asked to indicate which ones apply to the advertising. While this is useful in providing a measured profile of consumer response, it may lack the insight that qualitative research can provide.

Remember – view consumer/advertising interaction as a guide to how the advertising is likely to impact on the brand, not as an end in itself.

SUMMARY

- You are looking to assess the effect of advertising on the brand and consumer behaviour.
- Specific desired effects will be set by the brand situation/brand objectives.
- Brand effects will tend to be different for heavily functional brands as opposed to heavily emotional brands.
- Use appropriate research tools to measure brand effects and behaviour effects.
- Behaviour effects are generally seen in the short term (even if they also become long-term).
- Brand effects may be short-term or long-term.
- In all cases you are either looking for change or for stability.

Behaviour Measures (Short-Term)	
Simple Evaluation:	*Complex Evaluation:*
Direct (behaviour)	Observation
Indirect (sales)	Area Test
	Econometrics
Brand Measures	
Short-Term:	*Long-Term:*
Salience	Brand Health Check
Perceptions	Brand Attachment
Attachment	Brand Value
Consumer/ Advertising Interaction	

Part 2

ADVERTISING AGENCIES

Chapter 6
Advertising Agency Structure and Function

Whilst there are some minor variations in structure and function within advertising agencies, there are broad similarities in how the majority are organised. It is essential that who does what in an agency is understood if working relationships are to be optimised. In comparison with most marketing departments, the advertising agency structure seems rather complex. This apparent complexity reflects the fact that there is a lot more involved in pulling an advertising campaign together than first meets the eye.

In general the main departments in an advertising agency are as follows:

- account management;
- planning;
- creative;
- production (television/radio and print are usually two separate departments);
- media (may or may not be handled by the same agency);
- finance.

6.1 ACCOUNT MANAGEMENT

Account management is usually tiered in the following manner (the higher up the hierarchy, the more important the job is deemed to be!).

- Managing Director;
- Client Services Director;
- Account Group Head;
- Account Director;
- Account Manager/Supervisor;
- Account Executive.

The number of levels of account management will be determined by the size of the agency. Larger multinational agencies with large clients could employ all of these levels of management on a single account. Smaller agencies may only have a single person who fulfils the roles higher up the hierarchy.

The account management structure is flexible in that it can be tailored to suit the client to ensure that each level of a client's marketing department will have a natural point of contact with the advertising agency.

The function of account management is as follows.

- To liase with all departments within an advertising agency to ensure that the advertising campaign is developed to meet the client brief.
- To liase with the client during all stages of the advertising campaign development and implementation.
- To receive the client brief and reinterpret it into agency creative briefs and media briefs.
- To ensure that all work being developed within the agency on the client's behalf is being completed in a timely manner.
- To liase internally with all relevant departments to ensure that all parties are familiar with the status of the account.
- To present creative work to the client for approval and implement changes to the work that the client requests.
- To present production quotations and timing plans for client approval and ensure that the account is run smoothly.
- To be responsible for the account's profitability, including approving final billing to the client.

A good account person should become the client's 'business partner', responsible for generating profitable business for the agency and client alike. It is not uncommon for an account manager who develops a real empathy with a client's business to be approached to join the client's marketing department. For an account manager in an agency, this is perhaps the greatest accolade a client can give.

6.2 PLANNING

Planning was 'invented' in UK advertising agencies. Prior to the role of planning being formalised, agencies often had separate marketing intelligence and research departments. The planning department is an amalgam of these two functions.

Planners are recognised as being 'the conscience of the consumer', and the function of the planning department is as follows.

- To liase with the agency's account management and creative teams during all stages of advertising development and production.

- To liase with the relevant client departments to help in understanding the nature of the potential target audience, both behaviourally and attitudinally. These typically fall under the marketing, research and market intelligence departments.

- To understand and identify the market and consumer dynamics of a client's field of business fully.

- To identify the most appropriate target audience for the client's product or service.

- To understand and share the in-depth nature and typical behaviour patterns of the identified target audience. To develop the creative brief in conjunction with account management.

- To brief the creative department with account management.

- To liase with the creative department during all stages of creative development to ensure that work fulfils the requirements of the brief.

- To determine the necessity for research, both qualitative or quantitative.

- To select and brief outside research companies should research be necessary during the pre and post stages of advertising development.

6.3 CREATIVE

The creative department is usually headed up by the creative director, who is also often one of the agency's key representatives. The 'profile' of a creative director will often help determine the success or otherwise of the entire agency. The creative director is ultimately responsible for all creative work that his department produces and usually approves work before the client is given the chance to see it.

The creative director usually puts together creative teams who are in turn directed by a creative group head. The size of a creative group and the number that any agency may have is determined by the billings/workload of the agency. Creative teams are comprised of a copywriter and an art director who work together to produce the advertising proposals. Their functions are as follows.

Copywriter

- Determines all of the 'words' that are featured in an advertisement, e.g. headline and body copy in a press ad, the entire radio script, the dialogue of a television commercial.
- During advertising production, the copywriter briefs and approves the interpretation of the dialogue.

Art Director

- Is responsible for deciding the visual elements of an advertisement, e.g. pictures in a press ad, etc.
- During production, ensures that the work is being developed as intended, e.g. selecting photographers to shoot visual elements, selecting directors who can interpret a script as required.
- Acts as liaison during all stages of creative development to ensure the work is up to standard.

The roles of the art director and copywriter are not mutually exclusive – they should work as a team. Some creative teams enjoy and are encouraged to attend client meetings when their creative work is being discussed. Others prefer to stay firmly in the background.

6.4 PRODUCTION

The production departments within an agency are split into two separate units of press/print and television/radio.

Press and Print Production

Once the creative material has been approved by the client, the production department is responsible for ensuring that the ad is actually produced. The various functions within the department are as follows.

- ***Production head:*** oversees the entire department and is responsible for ensuring that all work is produced on time and within budget.

- ***Art buyer:*** liaises with the creative team to select outside suppliers who will provide input into the production of an ad, e.g. photographers, illustrators, etc. The art buyer is responsible for negotiating the fee for using this external talent.

- ***Typographer:*** selects the appropriate typeface in conjunction with the art director and ensures that the type layout is both legible and aesthetically pleasing.

- ***Progress:*** liaises with entire production department, creative department and account management to ensure that all of the elements of an ad are brought together for internal and client approval. Liaises with the media department to confirm bookings and ensure that material is dispatched to meet copy dates. The progress department is also responsible for ensuring the quality of the final reproduction of the printed material and producing production quotations for client approval.

Television and Radio Production

This department is led by the head of television who has teams of senior and junior producers working for him or her. The department head is ultimately responsible for the quality and financial control of his department.

The television producer's role is as follows.

- To liaise with creative teams to help select directors for television work.

- To negotiate and draw up quotations for all work produced.

- To ensure that all work is produced within the agreed budget.

- To liaise with the agreed production company to ensure a smooth production process.

- To book studios for recordings and post-production work on commercials.
- To ensure that the approved creative work is dispatched to the relevant stations to meet the airdate.

6.5 MEDIA

Media planning and buying is a function that is increasingly being handled by separate specialist buying units or companies which may or may not be associated with the creative/management function. The move to separate media companies has emerged as a result of increasing competition in the advertising world. During the early-1980s it was more commonplace for creative and media to be handled by a 'full service' agency. Now the most likely scenario is that companies wishing to advertise may appoint separate media and creative agencies. As media often forms the major part of advertising budgets, clients are often able to save money by using media buying agencies who are prepared to negotiate their commission levels. This will be discussed in more detail later in this chapter.

Most media departments are organised into a group of subsections that work closely together to plan and buy an advertising campaign. The departments most frequently found in agencies are as follows:

- planning;
- non-television buying (press, radio, posters, ancillary media);
- television buying;
- media research/intelligence.

Planning and Non-Television Buying

The media planner determines the shape and form of the media plan to reach the target audience in the most cost-effective way. From all of the media that are available, the options that are believed to represent the most sensible deployment of the client's budget will be selected. Through liaison with the account management, planning and creative teams, an achievable plan is put together.

In more specialist media buying companies it is likely that the planner will not negotiate and buy the media. This will be handled by further specialist buying departments.

The specific functions that a planner carries out are:

- comparing the quality and cost-effectiveness of all the potential media;
- calculating the coverage and frequency of the various media options;
- deciding on the best option for a balanced plan;
- putting a media plan together for client approval;
- informing production department of booked schedules to ensure that the appropriate creative material is produced to reach the copy deadline.

In companies where the planner is also responsible for media buying, they will obviously negotiate and book the proposed non-television media on receipt of client approval. In very small media companies the planning and buying role across all media is likely to be carried out by the same person.

In order to put an effective plan together, the media planner/buyer needs to have as much information as is available on the target audience. This information provides data on demographics, regionality, lifestyle information, seasonality, etc. This information provides the base rationale for any media plan. The client may provide some of this data or the planner/buyer may source it from the research department or from a relevant supplier.

Television Buyer

This is a very specialised role that is crucial to ensure that the client's budget is deployed most cost-effectively. The television buyer will:

- follow the planner's recommendations on the target audience to be reached and the media weight, coverage and frequency;
- liaise with the television buying groups/stations to negotiate the most efficient deal;
- book the television airtime;
- liaise with the account management/television production departments to ensure that commercials will be sent to the relevant stations to meet the airdate;

- ensure that the plan is fulfilled by checking through the campaign that the booked slots have been delivered to the audience as expected.

Media Research/Intelligence

Not all media departments or agencies have this department. Media research/intelligence is responsible for keeping the planners up to date with any audience research, media research, etc. that will help the planner to perform their role more efficiently. As the speed of change in the world of media continues apace, this role is becoming even more important.

Some agencies also employ a computer specialist who will carry out work on schedule and uses modelling as a predictive tool to help the department plan and buy more efficiently. Many media departments and agencies will brand their predictive modelling techniques and use them as an added incentive to retain or gain new business.

6.6 FINANCE

The client does not necessarily come into contact with the finance department, yet within the agency it has a very important role to play. The finance department:

- collates and distributes invoices for client payment;
- liaises with account management to ensure that the invoicing is sent out at the right time;
- prepares agency billing forecasts in conjunction with the account management department, which gives management the information on the potential income flow within the agency;
- ensures that client payment is made on time and in line with the contractual agreement.

6.7 APPOINTING AN ADVERTISING AGENCY

Appointing a new advertising agency can be a time consuming and daunting exercise. Some marketing personnel may never have to go through the agony of appointing a new agency, as many agency appointments are made due to international realignments over which local marketing departments have relatively little or no input.

For those in the position to be looking for a new agency, the management process comes to the fore. To choose the 'right' agency can change a brand's fortunes and set it off onto the path of fame and fortune. To make the wrong decision may result in low performance at best and potential disaster at the very worst.

There are many possible reasons why the pitch process may be set into operation. From reading trade press it would seem that the world of advertising is in a state of constant change. However, this is far from the truth. It is estimated that approximately 5-8 per cent of advertising expenditure changes hands each year.

Some of the reasons often given for looking for an agency are as follows.

- Strategic disagreements with the current agency on the direction that the advertising is taking.
- The current agency is judged to be under-performing.
- The current agency is unable to solve the creative problem, hence it is decided that a fresh creative approach is needed.
- An international network is needed.
- The current agency is too big and the account is not given enough attention.
- There is an account conflict; therefore, a new agency is required, as the agency may have resigned the business in favour of a more profitable competitor.
- New marketing management wish to change the advertising approach (the 'new broom syndrome').
- New to advertising with no current links to an agency.
- Desire for a full service agency, either media and creative, or an agency that can provide integrated communication solutions.
- Need a creative service or media-only agency in comparison with current full service offering.

Prior to undertaking a pitch, ISBA and the IPA recommend that the following points should be borne in mind:

- The selection and retention of the right agency is critical for an advertiser because of the key role that the advertising agency is able to play in promoting the company's brands and enhancing its ultimate profitability. Long-term relationships benefit the health of the brand. Try to make the existing relationship work rather than thinking that a move is necessarily the answer.
- If there is a requirement for a new advertising campaign, it will not always be right to pitch. An alternative is to approach an agency with whom the advertiser is already familiar, perhaps through work on another brand.
- If the advertiser proceeds to a pitch, it is not always appropriate to have a full creative pitch. Instead, strategic direction may suffice.
- Throughout the process of the pitch, both the advertiser and the agency need to be aware of material that is copyrighted and also of information and proposals which are highly confidential and are shared solely for the purpose of the pitch.
- The objective of the pitch process is to optimise the quality of response and the likelihood of selecting the ideal partner.
- Draw up a checklist of how you will be assessing the alternative pitches to score the competing agencies.

Assessing Competing Agencies

It is recommended to keep the decision-making team to as few people as possible, ideally comprised of only those directly responsible for advertising. If the decision-making team is too big, a compromise candidate is likely to win so that the best agency is not appointed, but rather the 'least worst'.

To eliminate subjectivity it is essential to have a structured assessment procedure to enforce rational rather than purely emotional judgement. The characteristics of your 'ideal' agency should be listed and allocated a weight. Agencies should be scored out of ten on each item on the assessment. The scores should be multiplied by the weighting and then totalled. By taking the scores of each of the members of the assessment team a final score for each agency is arrived at.

It is not automatic that the agency with the highest score should be appointed. Emotion still has a role to play. Members of the team have to assess if this feels like the right decision to appoint the agency in question. Proceedings can at this stage become somewhat unruly! Such a system is never going to be perfect, but it does help enhance the chance of making a better decision.

6.8 THE COMPETITIVE PITCH

The following is the 'Ten-Point Pitch Guide' recommended by ISBA and the IPA.

1. Prepare all the necessary background information.

- Prepare an outline brief.
- Consider the role of the advertising and other marketing communications and the potential contribution of the agency.
- Consider the type of agency required (e.g. in terms of size relative to budget, location, availability of international network and specialisation).
- Study the trade press.
- Identify relevant existing advertising which you rate highly.
- Talk to colleagues in other companies.
- Seek credentials information from, and possibly talk with, selected agencies that match the criteria in your outline brief. Be aware, however, of the dangers of information on your search becoming widely known.
- Approach ISBA and IPA for confidential information or detailed advice as appropriate.
- Finally, evaluate the information against your checklist.

2. Invite agencies to pitch.

- Decide on a positive list of up to three agencies only (four if incumbent is included).
- Don't be seduced into lengthening the list.
- Competing agencies should be aware of the number on the list.

3. Think of the response required and prepare a written brief accordingly.

- Prepare a concise but thorough written brief for the competing agencies.
- Identify and make clear all aspects on which the agency's presentation will be judged.
- It must be clear from the brief whether strategic proposals alone are required, or whether some creative ideas or a full pitch are expected. Agencies should respect the advertiser's wishes in this.
- Be explicit about the nature of the services that you expect to use.
- Indicate proposed remuneration and contract terms.

4. Consider the time necessary for a response to the brief.

- Prepare a firm timetable for the pitching process and stick to it.
- Time must be allowed for constructive ideas between brief and presentation.
- A four weeks minimum is suggested for work up to full creative pitch.

5. Help the process by demonstrating commitment with some financial contributions.

- The advertiser should decide whether to make a contribution to the pitch.
- Some financial contribution (announced upfront to all agencies on the short-list) shows commitment and the seriousness of your intent. The contribution is unlikely to cover all the costs, but the objective here is to motivate the agencies.

6. Give background data, interpretation and clarification.

- The advertiser should be willing to share market data and other relevant research on a confidential basis. The agency personnel should be allowed access to the people in the company with whom they would work if appointed.

- Ensure that there is a specified senior member of the advertiser's company to handle all enquiries and meet requests of the agency. Don't underestimate the time involved of someone being fully available over this time period.
- Allow the same rules of access to all those pitching.

7. Understand the roles of all those involved on both sides and set up an objective evaluation system.

- Ensure that all the decision-makers have been fully briefed and they are present at each pitch.
- Establish an objective evaluation system for assessing each pitch.
- Ensure that the agency presentation teams include people who will actually work on the business.
- Allow enough time (perhaps two days) for participants to attend, ask questions and discuss the presentations.

8. Insist on the necessary business disciplines before an appointment is made.

- Ensure that contracts and remuneration are discussed before an appointment is made.

9. Decide quickly and inform fairly.

- As soon as possible after the presentations (normally no more than one week), decide on the winning team. This may be extended if creative work is going to research.
- Establish a firm procedure for notifying both successful and unsuccessful agencies.
- Ensure that all pitching agencies are informed on the same day.
- Immediately issue a press release to the trade press.

10. Embrace the new agency into a long-term relationship and treat the losing agencies courteously.

- After the pitch, give the losing agencies the courtesy of a full 'lost order' meeting.

- Any losing agency must return all confidential material and information provided for the pitch to the advertiser. On request, the advertiser must return the losing pitch presentation.

- Honour the incumbent agency's contract, particularly with regard to agreed notice period and payment of outstanding invoices.

- Ensure that the incumbent co-operates fully in the handover to the new agency, making sure that all the advertiser's materials are handed back.

- Welcome the winning agency into the start of a long-lasting and mutually satisfying relationship.

6.9 APPRAISAL OF ADVERTISING AGENCIES

For most companies, appointing a new agency is not a practice that is carried out on a regular basis. To ensure that you continue to get the best out of your relationship with an agency, it is a worthwhile practice to review its work annually. This gives the agency an opportunity to 'show off' its work, or alternatively, it gives the client a forum to express any dissatisfaction with the way in which the account is currently being handled.

If there are any areas of dissatisfaction, it is not recommended to save them up for the annual review. What starts out as a small annoyance could become a major issue once a longer period of time has passed. Senior management should get involved to resolve issues if they are not easily 'fixed'.

This forum should be used as a dialogue with the agency and should not be seen as 'a stick'. The agency should be given an opportunity to comment on any areas of the working relationship with the advertiser and also suggest ways in which it could be improved if appropriate. The areas that should be reviewed will obviously be unique for each account, but are likely to be covered with the following checklist.

- **Senior agency management**: are they sufficiently involved?
- **Internal procedures**: are the 'systems' working as efficiently as possible?
- **Basis of remuneration**: is this still affordable? Are you getting value for money?
- **Legal and financial status**: is the agency still in good shape?
- **Other clients**: what has the agency track record been in attracting or losing business? What is the work like on other accounts (is it better or worse than the work on your account)?
- **Initiatives**: has the agency spontaneously inputted into any industry initiatives? Are these relevant to your account? Have any unprompted initiatives been taken on your account?
- **Quality and efficacy of your advertising**: are you happy with your ads or do you think that there is room for improvement? Be specific and give guidance on how you would like your advertising to be improved.
- **Creative department**: do you feel you have the commitment and involvement from this department? If appropriate, how evident is senior creative input?
- **Account management**: are they working well with the marketing department? Do they listen to you and incorporate your comments fairly? Do they seem in control of the account and genuinely know what is happening at all times?
- **Planning**: are you getting sufficient and relevant input from this department? Is their input evident in the quality of strategic thinking, the creative brief and research conducted on your behalf?
- **Media**: is the planning and buying as efficient as it might be? Have any initiatives been taken? Does the media department keep you informed of changes in the media market?
- **Through-the-line**: if the agency is operating through-the-line, are all departments communicating as well as they should? Does the work reflect this approach? If work is sourced from many agencies, are they liasing with the relevant parties?

- **Network:** if your agency is operating on an international basis, are they doing their job properly? Are all relevant parties kept in touch with developments on the account? Conversely, are you kept involved with developments on an international basis?

- **Personal compatibility with and professional capability of key members of staff:** this should be carried out for all of they key departments that are used, e.g. account management, creative, planning, media and production.

- **Any other relevant issues:** lastly, if you are happy with your agency's performance don't be afraid to say so. A little praise goes a long way.

6.10 AGENCY REMUNERATION

Agency remuneration negotiation can be an extremely technical and protracted affair, however, its importance cannot be underestimated. A well-negotiated arrangement results in a happy client who believes he is getting value for money and a happy agency who is operating a profitable business. This is sometimes overlooked by some clients who fail to understand that to optimise the working relationship with an agency, a profitable relationship for both agency and client must be part of the consideration. The skill in the negotiation is to incentivise the agency sufficiently to achieve your business goals whilst ensuring that the agency still remains profitable. Those clients who approach the remuneration process with the mentality that they will pay as little as possible are likely to have a far less fruitful and productive relationship with an agency. Clients don't necessarily like this truism about advertising remuneration, but nevertheless it should always be borne in mind during the negotiation process.

In the past, agencies were paid on a commission basis, i.e. a percentage of the income a client spent on media and advertising production was given to the agency as their income. The norm for commission levels in full service agencies was usually a non-negotiable 15 per cent of gross billings. This equated to 17.65 per cent of billings. The logic behind this system stated that the more a client spent, the more time an agency would have to devote to effectively servicing that account. Hence, a larger income would be needed to retain agency profitability.

This rather simplistic system has changed beyond recognition in the past twenty years.

Choosing the right remuneration package is now becoming an ever more complex process for a client. The key changes which have evolved in these income calculations are as follows.

Decline in Rates of Commission

The commission standard of 15 per cent is no longer an industry norm. Increased competition in the agency world has led to the decline in commission rates. The basic economic laws of supply and demand clearly operate in this field. The greater the number of advertising and media agencies that exist, the greater the competition will be between them. Reduction in commission can mean effective savings for a client. For example, a reduction from 15 per cent to 10 per cent represents a huge saving which can either lead to increased advertising expenditure or be put towards profitability. These commission negotiations play an extremely important role when changing agencies and even at the annual review level. There is no such thing as an agency norm. The right commission rate will be that which covers the agency servicing costs and allows them to make a reasonable profit on the account. Recent research by ISBA suggests that less than 4 per cent of all advertisers now pay 15 per cent commission.

The agency calculates the cost of servicing an account by calculating the man hour costs for all individuals who work on the account. These costs, along with an allowance for overheads, are combined and compared with the commission income resulting from projected annual expenditure. If agency costs exceed the income generated by an account, the result is an unprofitable account and vice versa.

The inherent danger with this system for some agencies, especially if media and production commissions are linked, is that it can put them in a financially precarious position if budgets are reduced significantly. Calculations for achievable profitability will have been made on the basis of a client spending a certain amount of money which is in his budget plans. If this expenditure fails to materialise, the results can sometimes be catastrophic for smaller agencies or those who are dependent on one or two large clients. For example, the agency develops a large volume of creative work on the basis that £10 million will be spent in December. A heavy investment of agency time has been made in the management and production of the creative product. This deficit has been planned to off-set the media commission income due in December to retain profitability on the account. The client, under pressure to increase his short-term profit, decides to reduce the planned expenditure from £10 million to £2 million. The result is retained profitability for the client but short-term financial disaster for the agency. Such precarious financial scenarios have resulted in the development of the fee system for the development of creative services whilst media negotiations remain largely commission based.

Fee System

With the devolution of the full service agency into creative and separate media planning/buying functions, with both operating a separate profit centre, it became clear that there would need to be a change in the way in which creative agencies were rewarded. Thus, the fee system was developed. This system of payment has been an industry standard for many related communication fields for some time, e.g. public relations, sales promotion. As media commission rates declined, due to the aforementioned competitiveness, a proportion of this saving has effectively been invested in the production of the advertising to be placed in the media.

The method of fee calculation involves assigning hourly rates to personnel on the basis of their salary and package costs and making an allowance for overheads. This annual total is divided into twelve, resulting in a guaranteed monthly income for the agency. Such developments have made financial planning of agencies somewhat less of a gamble. The only drawback for an agency is that if an account requires heavier levels of servicing than had been estimated (for example, due to problems with creative development), then the pre-negotiated fee may fail to cover the costs incurred on the account. The contractual arrangements drawn up will determine if the agency takes this loss or requests additional payment from the client to cover the unforeseen workload.

Payment by Results

Research published in early 1998 by ISBA[1] indicated that there has

---

1. ISBA, *Paying for Advertising: How Advertisers Remunerate their Agencies* (ISBA, January 1998).

been a marked shift towards this form of agency remuneration, usually as an agency incentive to increase their income. This research indicates that one in five of the advertisers surveyed now include this as an element of their agency remuneration packages.

The specialist accountancy firm Willott Kingston Smith has also conducted research[2] which also highlights the growth in importance of this form of remuneration. Of 100 agencies surveyed, who had combined billings of £1.6 billion, 41 per cent claimed that payment by results now formed a portion of their income calculations. This research also highlighted that it accounted for a very small proportion of the income in these agencies (less than 2 per cent).

This form of remuneration is likely to be of increasing importance to clients and agencies in the future, as agencies will be seen to have earned their reward. This is a classic win-win scenario – the client gets the results he desires and the agency gets a financial reward. The difficulty in ensuring the success of such a system will be in deciding the basis upon which performance will be measured. For some advertisers this may be relatively easy to calculate, e.g. a 2 per cent increase in sales during the period of advertising triggers the reward. Advertisers in this scenario must be guaranteed that nothing else changes in the marketplace, e.g. if the client is delisted from a major stocklist prior to the advertising, the advertising may be seen to have failed as the sales increase failed to materialise. In reality, though, the product was not available for purchase, and thus the client is at fault, not the agency.

If advertising objectives are set to shift attitudes then adequate research will need to be fielded, e.g. tracking studies to ensure that these shifts are monitored in the marketplace. Both agency and client must be clear and in agreement with the basis the advertising results will be measured by before entering into such an arrangement. In some agencies, it is also becoming common practice to split the performance-related element to reward the servicing of the account and the performance of the advertising as two separate elements. For example, if a 10 per cent performance-related bonus is given, then 5 per cent would be given on the basis of a good agency annual assessment and 5 per cent for achieving agreed sales targets.

---

2. Annual report on agency remuneration by Willott Kingston Smith (June 1996).

With the emergence of these differing methods of agency remuneration, contract negotiations have become ever more complex and are unlikely to be handled by marketing departments alone. It is common for financial, legal and specialist purchasing departments to be involved in this process.

Gone are the days of the straightforward commission deal for many clients. The move towards mixed methods of remuneration has arrived by combining elements of the aforementioned methods of income calculation. For example, some clients may pay for their media planning and buying on a commission basis and pay for their creative work on a monthly fee with a top up payment by results bonus.

For many companies, movements by many clients to monitor and audit media buying and production expenditure closely through the use of external and independent consultants has led to a more reliable way of ensuring that agencies are seen to be rewarded adequately and are not 'ripping off their clients'. Those agencies that manage their business responsibly have little to fear from such auditing. From a client's perspective, the only negative aspect of such close scrutiny of an agency's business is that an element of trust between the parties may be eroded. In addition, the cost of such auditing cannot be overlooked, as it can be a time consuming, and hence expensive, service for clients to commission.

Chapter 7
Developing an Agency Brief and the Briefing Process

The development and delivery of the agency brief is a crucial stage in the advertising production process. A single-minded, well-thoughtout brief which contains real consumer insight and is delivered in a motivating way will undoubtedly stand a better chance of producing great advertising. In comparison, a muddled brief hurriedly put together and faxed or e-mailed through to the agency is far less likely to succeed. The process of brief development should not be rushed – time and effort is needed to develop good briefs. They should not be dashed off, or even worse, repeated year after year.

Prior to the development of a brief, it is recommended that the first four stages of thinking outlined below are closely followed to ensure that the nature of the brand and the desired communication package is genuinely understood. Clients differ greatly in their approach to brief development. What I am about to recommend is an amalgam model that reflects the approach used by a variety of clients with whom I have been associated. This approach has usually resulted in good agency briefs being produced that have, in turn, had a greater success rate in producing outstanding creative work. The process of development is as follows:

1. Develop a statement of *brand essence.*
2. Develop a *brand positioning statement.*
3. Develop a *communication mix statement.*
4. Develop the *advertising brief.*
5. *Brief the agency.*
6. An *internal agency brief* is developed to brief the creative team.

This may appear to be a lengthy process, but it is an entirely logical way to tackle brief development. It ensures that the brand and its role is understood, and that the communication package in its totality has been thought through before that advertising brief is developed. The development of these elements is essentially free, as they are largely the responsibility of a client. Keep in mind that there will be an overlap between various elements on these documents, as they reflect a consistent approach being taken in defining the positioning of the brand.

7.1 BRAND ESSENCE

This is a process of distilling down the core elements that make up a brand. If this has not already been done or is not understood, it is recommended to define this document as a joint effort with the agency. This ensures that everyone involved in the creative development process is in agreement with what the brand stands for now, or is intended to stand for, in the future. This process is usually started by conducting a brand audit, followed by an informal workshop to pull all the thoughts together. It may also be necessary to use qualitative research to provide objective insight into brand composition. If it is left solely to marketing and advertising personnel to define the brand essence, there is the danger that their perspectives may not accurately reflect those of their target consumers.

The brand essence tool was designed to ensure that:
- everyone involved with the brand understands what is at its heart;
- the brand's unique values are communicated in the best and most powerful way;
- all brand activity is consistent with this unique essence.

The benefits of using the brand essence tool are:
- brand equity is strengthened over time;
- it provides a benchmark against which all work developed can be judged;
- it streamlines the process of identifying areas of possible brand extension;
- it enhances brand understanding to aid business growth;
- the development of a common language facilitates the sharing of ideas, insights, knowledge and teamwork.

There is no such thing as a 'Standard Brand Essence' concept. Individual agencies and clients have adapted and developed their own models to suit their individual requirements. This should be encouraged, as some elements of a brand essence need not necessarily be relevant to all brands. If personalised models are developed they are likely to be owned and used, as opposed to a model which is forced upon a client or agency and is seen to have little relevance.

Again, an amalgam approach is illustrated below, which represents most of the key elements that clients and agencies alike have found useful in better understanding the constituent elements of their brands.

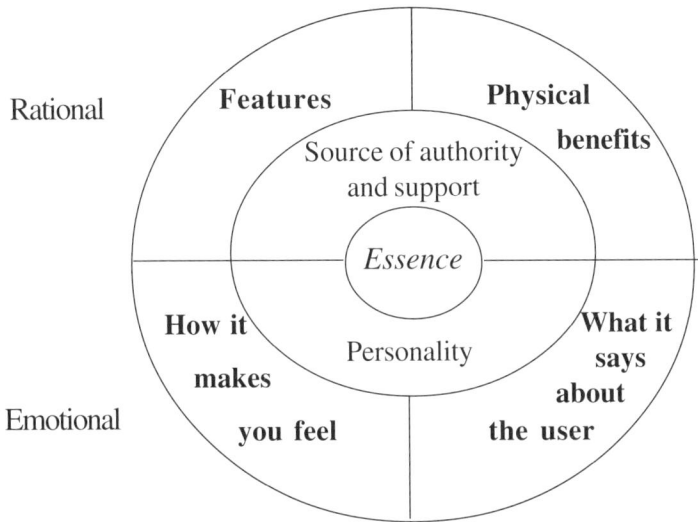

In order to understand a brand, it needs to be dissected in a fairly logical and precise manner. It is rather like looking at the layers of an onion. The outer layers represent those elements that are sometimes easier to articulate and understand, while the inner elements leading to the 'core' or heart of the brand are those unique facets of its personality that should be capable of setting the brand apart from the competition.

Outer Layers

- *Rational elements*

    Essentially, these help to understand the more rational elements of the brand, i.e. its rational features and the benefits that these attributes convey.

- **Emotional elements**

    These are the less tangible elements of the brand that reflect how it makes the consumer think and feel by using the brand and also how they think that they appear to the outside world through association with the brand. In other words, these are the emotional features and benefits (rational and emotional features and benefits are discussed in greater depth in Chapter 1).

Inner Layers

- **Source of authority and support**

    Any information should be included which provides reasons why the emotional and rational benefits can be claimed.

- **Brand personality**

    An understanding of the brand personality is needed. The easiest way of articulating this is to imagine them as a person or an inanimate object and then to describe them.

Core

At the heart of the brand essence is a distillation of the functional and emotional elements that are unique to that particular brand. For some brands this may be represented by a single word. For others, it may be a concise statement.

7.2 BRAND POSITIONING STATEMENT

This takes the understanding gained in the development of the brand essence a step further and moves closer to the information required in a creative brief. The brand positioning statement (BPS) is a detailed account of all those elements that relate to the brand. The information contained in the BPS comes from the brand essence and is a more detailed version of some of the information that appears later on in the agency brief. The BPS does not only relate to advertising; it is the statement of a brand's place in the market and applies equally to other elements in the communication mix. For example, if a direct mail campaign has been developed, it is essential that it remains true to the brand essence and BPS, or else the communication will cease to be integrated and may even be giving a fragmented picture of what the brand stands for. This can ultimately be very confusing for the consumer and is a wasteful way to deploy limited marketing budgets.

The BPS does not have to be written 'creatively'. It is a factual summation of the brand, its role in the market and how it relates to the consumer with a well-defined positioning. Typical headings on a BPS are as follows.

The Brand Positioning Statement Headings

- *Brand name:* statement of what it actually is and referral to what consumers call it if this is something different.

- *Brand description:* explanation of the physical attributes of the prouct.

- *Brand benefits:* those unique reasons why the brand fulfils a consumer need. These can be rational and/or emotional and should be taken from the brand essence.

- *Brand personality:* a description of the brand as if it were a person or other animate or inanimate object. This will also serve to differentiate the brand from others. This should be taken from the brand essence.

- *Brand core:* a distillation of the functional and emotional elements that are a unique to that particular brand, i.e. the 'heart and soul' of the brand. This is often best expressed in only one or two words, such as homeliness, indulgence, togetherness, refreshment, etc. This should be taken from the brand essence.

- *Differentiator:* this is an analysis of the brand's competitive advantage, or, in other words, what differentiates it from other competing brands. It may be taken from an insight or any of the rational or emotional benefits outlined above. There will normally be a close relationship with the brand's core. It should focus on the one or two key attributes/characteristics which will really differentiate the brand in the eyes of the specified target consumer. It is important to avoid 'throwing everything in for luck'.

The Market

- ***Market definition:*** description of the market/product category in which the brand competes. This should reflect the consumer's definition of the market/product category.

- ***Competitive set:*** description and analysis of the other brands contesting the same market/product category. A positioning map that shows how different brands relate by different characteristics is an excellent visual way to understand how the brand fits in against the competitors, and how/whether the competing brands are effectively differentiated. Again, this is extremely difficult to do for "corporate" brands that cover several market/product categories.

Consumer Target

This is described/analysed using three complementary approaches.

- ***Demographics:*** age, sex, income level, lifestage, level of education/qualifications, residence (area/type of residence, etc.).

- ***Psychographics:*** personality, attitudes, lifestyle, outlook, etc.

- ***Benefits sought:*** definition of the consumer's rational and/or emotional needs that the brand satisfies, such as what the benefits that the consumer seeks from the brand to satisfy the needs he/she feels are.

Further Supporting Analysis

- ***Consumer insights:*** exploring and analysing our consumer insight seeks to define the "truth in the brand", a fundamental belief that the consumer has about the brand (positive or negative) which has the potential to set it apart from the competition. This could provide a route to a competitive advantage/differentiation in subsequent communication with the target consumer, or indicate a substantial negative (real or imagined) which needs to be addressed, e.g. "It's the creamiest", "It's well built but too expensive", etc.

- ***Single-minded proposition:*** this is an expression of how the brand core and/or the differentiator can be made motivating, relevant and salient to the target consumer. It is an essential building block in the subsequent creative brief development process.

- *Supporting evidence:* this includes any performance-related or physical characteristics of the brand which provide rational supporting evidence as to how and why the proposition is relevant, motivating and distinctive.

Brand Positioning Summary Statement

This is a one sentence statement that draws together the stated brand proposition, the relevance of the brand to the target consumer and its essential source of differentiation. It acts as a final check that the previous analysis is internally consistent and provides a simple way of communicating the essence of the brand's positioning. In a sense it can be seen as a focused mission statement for the brand.

The BPS should always accompany all agency briefing with the brand essence, as they provide a more thorough background on the brand than a brief alone.

7.3 COMMUNICATION MIX STATEMENT

Advertising is an extremely important and potent communication tool, but it would be erroneous to suggest that it is the only one ever used. Most marketing organisations will use a combination of communication tools to work together to achieve a desired goal. It is too easy to develop and plan the use of a mixed communication package on an ad hoc basis. It is far better to plan the tools to be used and understand their relative roles at the beginning of a campaign planning process. This can be achieved by the development of a statement of the communication mix. The development of such a statement ensures that all activity will be planned and hopefully developed as a package, and that all those involved in the various elements of the communication plan have an understanding of the relative roles and weighting of the tools intended to be employed. A typical communication mix statement includes one or more of the following.

- ***Commercial strategy:*** summary of business objectives.

- ***Communication task:*** what change in attitude is needed to achieve any changes in consumer behaviour?

- ***Consumer task:*** statement of the behaviour change needed for the brand to grow.

- ***Communication mix:*** this should define the specific role and weighting of those communication tools that have been selected as elements of the communication plan. For example, the role of advertising is to increase awareness by x per cent, and will account for 50 per cent of the total expenditure.

- ***Key performance indicators:*** an indication should be made as to how the success of individual tools will be measured, e.g. sales response rates, shifts in awareness on a tracking study, etc.

Care should be taken when developing the communication mix statement to avoid a 'shopping list' approach. It is tempting to assume that all potential communication tools could be used. Unless the budget is large enough to support this diverse approach, it is likely that the plan could fail as the expenditure is spread too thinly, resulting in none of the tools achieving their desired objectives. The pros and cons of the potential tools are discussed in detail in Chapter 2.

This document and its explanation should be an integral part of any briefing process. It enables the agency to have a broader perspective of all planned activity on the brand.

7.4 CREATIVE BRIEF

Every new piece of advertising that is briefed should be accompanied by a new creative brief. If the rigorous three-step planning process outlined above has been adopted, it will be a much easier process to carry out in comparison with developing a creative brief without doing any of the thinking to develop a brand essence, BPS and communication mix statement.

It cannot be over-emphasised how important this piece of paper is in managing the advertising development process. The truism of 'garbage in garbage out' is never more relevant than when comparing the quality of the brief with the quality of the resultant creative output.

The creation of a brief demands time, intellectual rigour and exhaustive thinking. In essence, a good brief should be concise, comprehensible and, above all else, it should motivate the agency to give its best. The creative brief should always be accompanied by the brand essence, brand positioning statement and communication mix document.

The typical headings on an agency brief are as follows.

➢ *Reason for the brief.*

Be specific about why the brief is being given. For example, a change in the competitive focus means the current ad is now 'worn out'.

➢ *Aims and role of the advertising.*

Ideally, this should be summarised in one sentence to explain the effect that the advertising should be having on the target market in terms of its behaviour and attitude.

➢ *Target consumer.*

A summary of current and potential consumers should be given. This should always go beyond bald demographics. As much information as is thought appropriate should be included, drawing from all potential ways of segmenting consumers, e.g. sagacity, psychographics, etc. Some of the more successful briefs go as far as painting a portrait of the consumer, backed up with visualisation using pulls from magazines, etc.

➢ *What is the single-minded proposition?*

This must be single-minded to be effective. It should summarise what is unique about our brand and the benefit it brings to the consumer. In markets with parity products or in undifferentiated markets, it is usual to rely more heavily on emotional benefits or consumer insights to be distinguishable from the competition. This should not necessarily be expressed in creative or advertising language – that is the role of the agency creative brief, which is produced internally by the advertising agency. It is critical to identify one area that is unique that we can exploit, as this often becomes the driving force in advertising development.

➤ *Why can we claim this (support)?*

Be clear on providing reasons why the stated benefit can be claimed if this is appropriate. For purely emotional benefits it is less easy to include these, as they are usually more factually based pieces of information.

➤ *What is our personality?*

How are we currently viewed by current or potential consumers? Should this remain constant or do we wish to change? This information should be consistent with that developed in the brand essence.

➤ *Tone of voice.*

This states the type of personality you wish the advertising to adopt. This should reflect the personality statement made in the brand essence and BPS.

➤ *Advertising properties.*

Are we currently using any devices or properties that we wish to retain in the new advertising? Properties are as diverse as music, continuing characters, demonstrations, etc.

➤ *What is the budget?*

Provide best and worst scenarios if this is appropriate. Be honest about the budget level and also how safe it is likely to be.

➤ What is the timing?

Be honest about the first date that creative work is to be viewed and more importantly, when the on air or publication dates are that need to be met. If there are any additional time pressures, such as sales conferences, then supply this information as well.

➤ Media.

If there are preferred media, this should be stated. The final media proposals will result from the separate media brief that should be developed and briefed at the same time as the creative brief. This is discussed in greater detail in Chapter 11.

➤ Evaluation criteria.

Be clear on how the creative work will be assessed before and after production, such as qualitative research to assess initial proposals, etc.

7.5 TOWARDS THE PERFECT BRIEF

It has been acknowledged that developing a good creative brief can be an involved and complex process. The following may provide some practical ideas that will help perfect the brief development process.

➤ Work together to prepare the brief.

The process of preparing a brief for advertising is complex. It calls for the assimilation of vast amounts of data and knowledge into a cogent, comprehensive document. This should ideally be a joint process. Some of the best briefs result from a pooling of resources between both the client and agency to develop the brief together. It is usually the responsibility of the client to prepare the final brief, but always involve the agency in all stages of its conception and preparation.

➤ *Look for new ways of thinking about the brief.*

The ultimate purpose of a brief is the agreement by the agency and client on the best direction in which to guide the creative team to meet the objectives of the brief. On reading the brief/creative strategy, the creative team should feel equipped to express a brand's benefits in a unique and relevant advertising approach.

Try to avoid repeating briefs time after time. There will have been changes in the market and the brief should reflect these. Any breakthrough in thinking, new insights and perspectives on the brand and what it means to the consumer will help channel the creative process more effectively. If there are leaps in understanding made at the briefing stage, it is also more likely that there will be a leap in the conceptual development and the resultant creative work.

➤ *Look for a focus.*

The more focused a brief is, the better the resultant creative work is likely to be. Poor briefs are characterised by being rambling, unfocused, include too much or irrelevant information and may even fail to address the key issues.

➤ *Summarise your aims succinctly.*

The acid test of a good brief is to be able to summarise it in one sentence. The sentence must explain what effect the advertising must have on the target's attitudes and behaviour.

➤ *Decide what the communication issues are.*

Prior to developing a brief, all parties need to be clear on the communication issues relating to the brand as they currently stand. For example:
- What is the 'big idea' in the current advertising?
- Does this 'big idea' work?
- Can the 'big idea' be developed?
- Do we need a new strategic approach?

> *Be clear on where you are now.*

You should be clear on where you see the brand positioning and brand objectives. Ask the agency to conduct a similar exercise to see if there is agreement or disagreement on these issues. Pooling information on the brand will enable you to form a cohesive summary of market dynamics, consumer culture and the visual and communication issues that effect the brand.

If possible, after the consultation with the agency, a formal summary of the brand's current status should be drawn up and agreed on by all parties in the form of the brand positioning statement. If the four-stage process outlined in this chapter is followed, there should not be any doubt on the current status of the brand.

> *Be clear on the 'brand vision'.*

Decide where you want the brand to be in the future. Without a vision, you will be unable to plan the steps that you need to go through to fulfil the brand ambitions. The development of the brief represents a culmination of the strategic thinking process outlined in Chapter 2. This involves understanding how the brand fits into the marketing concept, refining information gathered in the strategic trawl, recognising the importance of integration in the communication mix statement and finally, drawing all the information gathered in the brand essence and BPS into a coherent advertising agency brief.

Such a thorough process helps ensure that the correct brief is being given to the agency. To repeat the information outlined in Chapter 2, this is the last piece of documentation to be prepared. It cannot be done in isolation or without preparation of all the background material outlined in Chapters 2 and 7.

7.6 THE BRIEFING MEETING

This is the next critical stage in the management of the advertising development process. The meeting should be as inspirational as the brief itself. The result at the end of a good briefing meeting should be a highly motivated agency team who are clear and in total agreement with the vision you have for the brand communication. Handling meetings is a very individual process; nevertheless, there are some clear guidelines that will help ensure that the briefing meeting goes as smoothly as possible.

➢ *Have the core team present.*

The core agency and client team should be present for all major creative briefings. From the agency side, at the absolute minimum the account team and planner should be briefed. If possible, insist on having the creative team present. Some agencies refuse to field these personnel in a face to face setting with clients, whilst others are happy to do so. To ensure that all members of the communication team are kept abreast of developments, it may be advisable to have a media planner present. The media brief can also be delivered at this meeting.

➢ *Share your brief development.*

Take the agency through your flow of logic from the brand essence to brand positioning statement through to the communication mix and finally your brief. The agency will have the total picture and, assuming the brief is a good one, they can understand the brief in totality.

➢ *Give the meeting a focus and a theme.*

At the beginning of the meeting, clearly set up the purpose of the meeting and the vision for the brand. This should be set apart and markedly different in tone to 'just another meeting with the agency'.

➢ *Be inspirational in the way you handle the meeting – bring the product and benefit alive.*

Be excited about your brand. Think of different ways in which you could handle the meeting. If you are advertising a restaurant, hold the briefing meeting in situ to make the brand experience come alive. There is a notorious agency legend of a briefing for a brand of swimwear which was held in a jacuzzi with all team members wearing the product. Even the briefing document was laminated to prevent the paperwork getting unnecessarily waterlogged. This type of inspired presentation will undoubtedly enthuse the agency.

The brand should be available to be used, touched, felt, tasted, etc. Try and bring the benefit alive in as relevant a way as possible. It is through such inspirational briefing that the creative process begins.

> *Visualise the target.*

Go beyond the bald demographics and more interesting psychographics. Put together 'mood boards' to represent your target. These are essentially visuals from magazines that could portray your consumers, their lifestyle, where they live, etc. These are portrayed in a visually interesting way to bring the target to life. In a similar fashion, it may also be useful to explain who you are not targeting in order to clarify the target.

> *Stick to the brief.*

During the course of the meeting, which may be a nerve-racking process, it is easy to ad lib and move away from the brief. Stay as close to the brief as possible. Nuances of language can result in confusion and the brief being misinterpreted.

> *Answer questions delivered to you.*

You are likely to be questioned closely by the agency, usually to clarify points made. Ensure that all questions are clearly answered. Don't be belligerent if your brief is challenged. This can greatly effect the mood and direction of the briefing meeting. If the agency is challenging your brief, they may be doing so with good reason. Listen to their point of view.

➢ *Sum up the meeting and agree on the next steps.*

This is your meeting and you will be expected to run it efficiently. Sum up any amendments or changes that have been agreed upon during the course of discussion. The next steps and timing should be agreed on at this stage.

7.7 THE INTERNAL AGENCY CREATIVE BRIEF

Following your briefing, the agency account team and planner of your brief translate it into an agency creative brief. If your thinking is sound and innovative, you may find that the creative brief bears a striking resemblance to your own brief! The creative brief often seeks to take your thinking one stage further in the creative development process.

Most clients are given the opportunity to approve a creative brief prior to it being given to a creative team to work on. This is often a useful safety check to make sure that your brief has not been misinterpreted. A typical briefing format is illustrated by the creative brief summary checklist presented below.

- What job are we trying to do?
- Who are we talking to?
- What do we want them to think when they see the ads?
- Proposition.
- Support.
- Tone of voice.
- Guidelines and mandatories.
- Media and budget.

When given an opportunity to approve the brief, it is useful to ask yourself the following questions to ensure that it meets your requirements:

- Is it true to your brief?
- Is it focused?
- Is the proposition single-minded?
- Do you believe the support?
- Can you visualise the target?
- Has enough or too much time been allowed for development?
- Have the mandatories been included?
- Has it been made clear how the advertising will be evaluated?

On completion of this process the agency will now be ready to start the creative development process in earnest.

Chapter 8
Making the Client/Agency Relationship Work

Why do some clients appear to have fantastically successful relationships with their agencies while others seem to be in a constant state of turmoil and dissatisfaction, and the majority float somewhere between these two extremes? Are there any rules or guidelines that can help ensure that relationships with agencies are always as fruitful as possible?

Each client and agency relationship is likely to be unique, hence it is difficult to give hard and fast rules that could be applied across the board. Some agencies and clients refer to their relationship as 'a marriage'. This is probably a good analogy. The relationship is not always going to be a bed of roses but those partners who work at their 'marriage' are likely to have a greater chance of succeeding.

As there are always two sides to every story it is best to look at the relationship from both an agency and a client perspective. What do both parties expect of each other and what would both like to see happen in the relationship to make it a good one? *(NB* The agency perspective has been written by an agency person and the client perspective by a client.)

8.1 THE AGENCY PERSPECTIVE: WHAT CONTRIBUTES TOWARDS A GOOD CLIENT RELATIONSHIP?

Timing

➢ *Allow enough time.*

This is often a critical element which can have major repercussions on creative development and the quality of the final creative work. The golden rule is that there is never enough time, so clients should plan accordingly! Allow as much time as possible for creative development. See Chapter 4 for further details on this.

➢ *Be honest about timing.*

Clients should always be honest about timing. Imposing false deadlines can often be counterproductive and can affect the basic integrity and honesty of working relationships with agencies. It may provide a short-term solution to satisfy the client desire to see creative work but be aware that excellent creative work is unlikely to result as it usually takes longer than 24 hours to come up with a great idea.

➢ *Stick to timing plans.*

The client as well as the agency should try to stick to the timing plans. If there are likely to be problems, e.g. clients unavailable to approve work at the specified time, it is important to let the agency know as quickly as possible.

Briefing

➢ *Be inspirational.*

The more clients put into briefs and briefing the better the finished creative work is likely to be. Chapter 7 gives further detail on this point.

➢ *Be thorough.*

Make sure that enough time and effort has been given to develop the brief. Following the procedures outlined in Chapter 7 will help ensure that this is optimised.

➢ *Listen to the agency.*

Try not to be too sensitive if the agency questions a brief. They may have spotted unforeseen flaws in your arguments. Be open to the points they raise. A better brief may even be the result of their comments.

Creative Judgement

➤ *Time.*

Allow enough time and 'mental space' to assess creative work effectively. Very few clients are gifted enough to give a reasoned, logical response with three minutes' thought. Clients should not be afraid to ask for 24 hours before formally responding if this makes for better decisions. From a personal credibility point of view a delayed response may allow clients to reflect the comments of all involved in the advertising development process rather than the all too familiar occurrence of brand management 'buying' an idea only to find that a more senior person rejects the work. When this 'buy/non-buy' scenario occurs it is extremely demotivating for the agency, and this can affect the quality of the working relationship. If a delayed response is to be used make the agency aware of this at the time of briefing so that it does not come as a complete shock.

➤ *Be brave.*

Creative work that scares clients is often a good thing. Bravery in decision-making usually results in better creative work that will have a chance to impact on its audience. Retreating to safety and familiarity can result in work that is neither outstanding nor impactful.

➤ *Have an open mind.*

Before being presented with creative work clients should endeavour to keep an open mind. The tendency is for clients to have already mentally written the creative work, which can often cloud their judgement when presented with the creative work. Objectivity should always be obeyed at all times.

➤ *Be honest.*

If the creative work is not suitable, for whatever reason, clients should be honest and say so. Don't waste agency time and energy by requesting amendment after amendment and then reject it because 'it will never work'. Honesty at all times from a client will gain respect from the agency in the long run.

> *Push the agency to achieve more.*

If clients feel that the work is not good enough they should push the agency for an alternative. This may prove uncomfortable in the short term but if better creative work is the result the agency will be grateful in the longer term.

> *Give direction if you reject creative work.*

When creative work is rejected always give a well-argued rationale as to why it is not suitable and provide direction and motivation to take the creative development process to the next stage. Clients should never reject work purely on the basis that they 'don't like it' or it 'doesn't grab them'. Agencies need more direction than this to produce work which will be suitable.

> *Be knowledgeable about advertising.*

Take time to be aware of new advertising campaigns by either being an alert consumer or by regularly reviewing current advertising, e.g. monthly competitive reels, trade press, etc. The more the client can immerse themselves in advertising and have comments to make about campaigns, the better their creative judgement is likely to be. Most people in marketing and advertising love talking about adverts, so this should not be hard for good clients to do.

Administration

> *Be honest about your budgets and any likely changes.*

If there is any doubt that a planned budget may fail to materialise, the agency should be made aware of this risk as soon as possible. The financial planning of an agency could be dependent on such information, so in the interests of professionalism it is only fair to provide fair warning if budgets are likely to be reduced or cut altogether.

Teamwork

> ***Work with the agency during development of communication plans.***

Total communication with the agency during all stages of campaign development will greatly enhance the working relationship. Involve the agency right at the beginning of the planning process – start with the new product development brief so that they are aware of all the steps in bringing a product to market.

> ***Ask for help.***

Clients are often surprised when agencies can provide solutions to business problems unrelated to communication issues. Agency staff often have diverse portfolios of accounts that they work on, and as a result often have both a breadth and depth of knowledge that clients may be unaware of. Share your problems with the agency – they may not always provide solutions, but it improves the working relationship as the agency will feel a valued member of the 'team'.

> ***Business partner approach.***

Agencies are your business partners, not slaves to source tickets to the Cup Final! Both parties seek a profitable working relationship, and this should never be lost sight of. Agencies wish to help clients achieve their business objectives, and in so doing will build themselves a healthy and profitable business. The attitude of partnership is incredibly important if clients are to get the most out of an agency.

> ***Have fun and retain a sense of humour.***

The marketing function has some elements to it which are quite frankly a bit dull. Admittedly, advertising development can sometimes be a problematical process, but it can also be fun. Try to enjoy it. Enthusiastic and fun from clients make for fruitful relationships with agencies. Dull, inward-looking clients who lack a sense of humour are likely to gain less from their working relationships with agencies. By showing such 'human' characteristics, the agency can begin to develop a more personal relationship with you which greatly enhances the working relationship.

8.2 THE CLIENT PERSPECTIVE: WHAT CONTRIBUTES TO A GOOD AGENCY RELATIONSHIP?

Understanding the Client's Business

➢ *Understand the business context.*

An agency should always demonstrate that it understands the client's business context. Whilst in the end advertising has to engage the consumer, it should not be approached as a pure art form. The marketing team in a business is always under pressure to demonstrate the value that advertising adds. Advertising is often the single biggest investment a company may make, yet measuring the return on investment is often difficult. An agency that demonstrates an understanding of financial targets/constraints of a client will find the client more receptive to its creative solutions.

➢ *Understand the way the client works.*

Every company works under different rules and procedures. It is critical that the agency understands those that relate to how the client manages advertising. This covers sign-off and briefing procedures. For example, if a brief requires a senior manager's sign-off, the agency will save itself time and hassle by refusing to accept a brief issued by a junior manager. Whilst it is true to say that all companies operate by different rules, it is also fair to say that most companies bypass their own rules dependent on the exigencies of the business. Whilst the written rule may be that the marketing director has to approve all the advertising at script stage, it may be that in certain cases he may delegate this to a particularly able manager. Conversely, whilst it may be the written rule that the marketing director has the final sign-off, there are companies where, in reality, the chairman's wife has the final say!

The agency should thus make a point of determining who the key decision-maker(s) are (both formally and informally), and ensure that they 'buy in' at the critical stages.

Strategic Thinking

> *Stimulate the client to develop long-term thinking.*

As we have previously said, the client is more likely to be focused on the delivery of short-term results, and much of the client's thinking around strategy will be done referencing past data. The agency has a valuable role to play in stimulating new thinking about what the future may hold. The agency has access to a far broader data set than its individual clients, and since the agency's success relies on generating difference and newness in communication, its data tends to be more predictive than that of a client. Agencies which have vision and take the initiative for their clients on a regular basis by using different sources of stimulus can make themselves almost indispensable to a client.

> *Provide a competitive perspective.*

The client will be very focused not only on his own performance, but also on the performance of his competitors. Usually the client's analysis will be based around the business results of his competitor. The agency can add real value by analysing the competition from an advertising perspective. What advertising/communication strategies are they adopting? What are their campaign platforms and the implications for the client's advertising/media strategy, etc?

> *Find space to create an environment for 'blue sky' thinking.*

Clients often find it hard to break away from the day to day pressures of the business in order to focus on developing advertising. The need to deliver the weekly sales will always take precedence. A good tip for the agency is to ensure that the key creative/planning response meetings are held away from the client's workplace, ideally at the agency. It is more difficult for the client to be tracked down by his boss/sales team if he is away from the office. Also, it generally means that the client arrives at the agency in a more focused frame of mind. This is likely to result in a higher quality of input from the client.

> ➢ *Bring objectivity and a broader view.*

A client's knowledge base is always referenced to its own sphere of operations and is therefore somewhat limited. Through its work on other accounts, the agency can help broaden and deepen its client's understanding of both its current and potential target consumers. The agency should also challenge the client's 'sacred cows'. It is easier for the client to preserve the 'status quo', therefore, the agency should draw on its knowledge base to provide deeper insights into the benefits of taking the radical option.

Creative Process

> ➢ *Bring the idea to life.*

Much analysis has been done on the great advertising campaigns as to why and how they generated the consumer reaction that they did. During earlier stages of creative production, a discussion as to how the client was able to spot the potential of the idea would be equally interesting. Much creative material presented by agency teams 'tick the boxes' in meeting the client brief, yet to the dismay of the creative team who thought up the creative idea, the client fails to see the fully formed creative idea as the creative conceived it. No client is going to approve the idea on the basis of 'trust us, it all comes down to the casting, filmic style, photographers' input, fab location', etc. Agencies can help the approval process enormously by thinking about how to best visualise and present the idea in the absence of the finished article.

> ➢ *Art for art's sake.*

Many a budding writer/film director has started their career in advertising. However, the agency needs to remember that the advertising, whilst more likely to prove effective if it entertains and involves the target, is in the end designed to generate more sales. The agency must ensure that the creative idea does not overwhelm the client's key advertising message.

Administration

> ### *Keep the client informed.*

Once the creative work has been approved, it is important that the agency keeps the client well briefed on the status of the work. The production process often involves a series of highly technical steps with different timescales and levels of cost associated with them. Having agreed an overall budget with the client, the agency should help the client to navigate their way through the resulting work. Keeping the client in touch during the stages of production will ensure that there are no nasty surprises or missed opportunities to make appropriate changes, which is likely to happen if the client has been kept unaware of the status of the work.

> ### *Make production costs clear.*

The agency should make sure that the costs of production are clearly understood by the client. Again, the client does not have a high level of expertise on the technical aspects of advertising production, so the agency should make the estimates as clear and simple as possible. It is not conducive to good agency relations for the agency to produce additional estimates half-way through a production process unless there have been genuine unforeseen circumstances. The danger with such extra charges is that the client will be unlikely to have budgeted for them.

SUMMARY

From both the agency *and* client viewpoint there is a fair degree of consistency in what each side would like to see from the other. In essence, both sides are ultimately striving for the same end result: the best creative product that stands the best chance in the marketplace of achieving the objectives of the client. Problems with the working relationship occur not because this larger goal has been forgotten, but because the minutiae of detail and the complexity of the development and production process somehow becomes so intrusive that the collective eyes of both client and agency can be, metaphorically, taken off the ball.

It takes good management practice from both client and agency to make sure that the previously discussed 'hassle factors' are minimised and the best practice put into place to effectively and efficiently produce great creative work. Whilst the role of the creative department should never be underestimated, it is essentially a joint client and agency management function that drives this whole process. If management commitment or ability is lacking from either partner, the result is likely to be a less than fruitful outcome. With coherent and complementary management styles, the chances of a profitable outcome for all are far more likely.

Part 3

PRACTICAL APPLICATIONS

Chapter 9
Understanding Creative Work

Why is understanding creativity so difficult? What's the problem? These are a creative person's favourite questions, yet they are the questions we all ask when we're trying to be helpful, the questions we ask ourselves whenever we're trying to assess a situation and resolve our next action. So when we answer these questions are we being creative? To some extent yes, but advertising creativity is more complex.

An advertising idea has to communicate itself, not just simply exist. You might say it's not an idea unless someone else understands it. You would be right to say it's not a good idea unless it moves the recipient to action or to purchase the product.

For many people, "What's the problem?" is far easier to answer than "What's creativity?" Creativity requires both *freedom* to cover all the options and *discipline* to focus on the parameters of the specific problem. You could describe this as 'freedom within a framework'. The discipline is liberating.

We all know the difficulty of confronting the blank sheet of paper. With an open brief it's much harder to even make a mark, let alone have an idea. A tighter brief focuses your brain on a specific problem. Our brain is divided into two halves with separate functions. Discipline and freedom could be the sub-headings for the left and right brain.

Discipline	**Freedom**
Rational	Intuitive
Sequential	Multiple
Analytic	Holistic
Objective	Subjective
Intellect	Emotion
Logic	Random
Reason	Anarchy

To be creative, you have to use *both* halves of your brain. Imagine there is a gap between the two halves. Both sides of that gap are a series of pigeon holes. The left-hand side's holes are arranged in a logical, ordered fashion. The right-hand side is random and intuitive. Subjects don't always line up. A creative person happily releases pigeons from either side of that gap, intrigued to see which hole they choose to settle in on the opposite side.

We often talk about the creative leap. The pigeons are a metaphor for that expression and, as we'll see, metaphors are frequently used in creative ideas.

9.1 DEFINING AN IDEA

The dictionary tells us that 'to create' means 'to bring into being'. In advertising terms, creativity must also communicate and be relevant. You could argue that creativity must see something in a new way and be able to articulate and communicate that insight in an arresting and stimulating manner.

Jokes are a good example of creativity, often turning things on their head to make a point. They begin by taking something familiar and then showing it to you in a different light. Yet, for the joke to work, it has to have an inner logic. Let's take a look at this joke as an example: *An old prawn went to a disco, but all he pulled was a mussel.*

'Old prawn' is the clue, 'pulled' is the double meaning that sets up the final word 'mussel', the double meaning of which creates a smile when we 'get it'. Creating an idea works the same way. For it to work, you have to be able to find your way back from the idea as it is expressed in the advertisement to its origin.

For the creative person, this is a good check. A thought is translated into an idea. If the idea is accurate, it should be possible to translate back to the original thought.

Ideas aren't difficult to recognise, but what are they? In most cases, there are two elements in an idea – verbal and visual. Essentially, an idea is the sudden marriage of the two thoughts that were not perceived to have any relationship before their union.

Advertising creatives use this 'twoness' in many ways, using an outside element to compare, contrast, substitute for or combine with their product to create an idea. Look for the 'twoness' in a selection of advertisements. You'll be surprised how easy it is to spot. However, don't be fooled – spotting is one thing; making the initial connection is the difficult part of being creative.

Now that we understand something of what an idea is, how do you have one? Creatives will tell you that you can't have an idea, they just happen. Yet you can create an environment where ideas are more likely.

Compare the creative environment with an office. The office is focused around the desk, the computer, perhaps a meeting table. The creative environment is full of distractions: visual stimuli on the walls, a sofa, scribbles on the floor, an overflowing wastepaper basket, music playing. The first is the home of the left brain, the second home of the right.

The words 'creative' and 'office' are so separated in *Roget's Thesaurus* that you're more likely to be able to perceive a connection between 'laid back' and 'industrious'.

Oddly, the connection could be the *creative office*:

- There's a lot of clutter (laid-back).
- There's a lot going on (industrious).
- There are no clues to authority or hierarchy (unless you notice the awards).
- No one has positioned the desk to give themselves an advantage, nor does anyone feel the need to suggest 'here sits an analytical or logical mind'.
- The desk isn't where creatives automatically do work. It's where work accumulates (some might say 'breeds').
- It's a place where, just by the accident of being side by side, thoughts collide.

We have all experienced the 'having an idea in the bath' syndrome. Creatives are the first to admit ideas happen in 'off' moments, when the mind is in limbo. Creativity isn't nine to five. If only it was, creatives could clock in, have an idea and clock out. It doesn't look like work, but when a creative has their feet up staring blankly out of the window, they're hard at it.

Arthur Koestler, writer and philosopher, said, "The unconscious is a breeding ground for novelties." When travel writer Jan Morris arrives in a new foreign city, she spends the first day wandering around in what she calls "productive indolence". Now that's certainly one way creatives explore the brief – they've just never had a phrase for the paradox before.

"Productive indolence" also exhibits 'twoness'. The two words contrast and become an idea expressing exactly what Jan meant.

9.2 THE CREATIVE PROCESS

Creatives learn to put their mind in a receptive state. After all, 'chance favours the prepared mind'. You won't find many creatives who've been in the Boy Scouts, but they all know the motto "be prepared". For our purposes, this is made easier by following this five-step process:

1. **Preparation.**
    This is the beginning of the creative process and can take many forms. Background reading is important, but not just the conventional library or Internet visit. More gems are to be found in the specialist magazines of the target market. Background experience is also essential. Meeting the consumer on their own ground will be invaluable as far as language, tone of voice or other interests are concerned.

    Interrogation is also part of preparation. The agency planner, a vital player in the creative process, will be quizzed at how he arrived at the creative brief. Assumptions will be questioned. And don't forget the factory visit. Many a creative 'nugget' has been mined on a trip to the production line.

    This period can be described as 'creative person as sponge', indiscriminately soaking up anything and everything.

2. **Frustration.**
    Frustration is positive. If you're frustrated it means you've made a false assumption, gone up a blind alley. Retrace your steps, find out where you went wrong. Panic even. "All that preparation and no idea. What a waste of time. Sod it, I'm going to take a break, walk the dog, have a bath."

3. Incubation.

Playing off the ball, playing hooky, playing with the soap – they are all legitimate activities during incubation. Both the conscious and the subconscious are involved.

'Productive indolence' only happens when the brain is in neutral. Thoughts collide when the mind is in free fall.

This ability to disengage, often when under deadline pressure, is a skill that has to be learnt the hard way. It takes experience to have the conficence to 'chill out'.

Yet we all know how it works. How often have we said, "I just had an idea. I've no idea where it came from, but...". That is the moment of transition to the next stage, insight.

4. Insight.

This is the moment of inspiration, of connection. It is no coincidence that, visually, ideas are shown as happening by a light bulb coming on above someone's head.

Seeing the light is as instant as flicking a switch, not a leap in the dark, but rather, a creative leap. Ideas rarely emerge fully formed but we can all recognise the moment the penny dropped. "It just came into my head" is what we say when asked to explain ourselves.

The fact that there are so many colluquial expressions for 'the moment of truth' shows the air of mystery surrounding idea generation.

The fascinating thing is that no matter how many times a creative goes through this process, it's never the same. The plan is to keep preparation and incubation down to a minimum and head straight for the insight. Each can last seconds, days or weeks. There are no guarantees. All this makes producing timing plans and budgets for this process one of the less exact sciences. When the insight must be shared, it brings us to the final stage, presentation.

5. Presentation.

At this point, good creatives return to the brief. They may ask questions such as, "Does it fit?", "Have I missed anything?", "Have I expressed it in the right way?", "Is it interesting, arresting, intriguing?" These are all big questions, and act as trip wires for a poorly thoughtout idea.

Now you can see what an idea goes through before becoming an advertisement seen by a client. It's a fragile process, but it's also exciting and exhilarating. You can also see why the creatives refer to their idea as their 'baby'.

It's important for a client to be good at rearing these 'children' rather than killing off creatives' ideas. No one wants to be thought of as 'the advertising assassin', so how do we judge creative work?

9.3 JUDGING CREATIVE WORK

When judging creative work, we begin at the end with the consumer, the person whose loyalty the advertisement has to earn. For clients to understand how to judge creative work, they must first understand how a consumer reacts to an advertisement.

Consumers often ask the same questions as clients, but they express them differently. A typical consumer reaction on seeing an ad might be, "I'm in a hurry and you're not the only one wanting to talk to me, so why should I give you my valuable time?" A client may not express it the same way, but the question is essentially the same. "Is the ad arresting?", "Will it stand out?", "Is the consumer benefit obvious enough?"

When dealing with creative people, it is useful to pose questions from the consumer's point of view. It's the same question but far less aggressive and less confrontational.

Below is a number of other possible consumer and client responses.

Consumer: Do I know you? What did you say you're called?
Client: Is the branding strong enough?

Consumer: Do I like you?
Client: Are we too aggressive? Is the tone of voice right?

Consumer: Are you sure you understand me?
Client: Is the insight correct for our target market?

Consumer:	*OK, so what's in it for me?*
Client:	*How obvious and relevant is the end benefit?*
Consumer:	*What are you trying to tell me?*
Client:	*How clear is our message?*
Consumer:	*Why should I trust you?*
Client:	*Is this credible? Does it support our core values?*

Whatever the question, the consumer's response is instinctive, spontaneous and affected by time, place and circumstances. Clients can't afford to behave like that. Their judgement process has to be more analytical. Personal preference is a dangerous tool. Present creative work to two different people and you'll get two different reactions, unless those people have some guidelines that they both respect.

How can clients be fair, constructive and part of the recognition and protection process? Sadly, there are no Ten Commandments for this area, but over time a number of guidelines have emerged as being present in most of the advertisements that are deemed successful.

When a parent finds a child up to no good, they often ask, "What's the big idea?" It's the first question a client should ask themselves when viewing creative work. Without one coherent idea, the ad is up to no good. They should also ask the agency. Unless they both agree on the expression of the 'big idea', the two parties will be talking at cross-purposes.

Look at the ads you admire, and you'll notice that the one thing they all have in common is single-mindedness. That one 'big idea' will also need to be connected to the brand.

For Volkswagen, the big idea is 'reliability'. To launch the Beetle in America back in the 1960s, they asked the question, "How does the man who drives the snowplough get to the snowplough?" You've guessed the answer already, the car you can rely on to start first time, the Volkswagen Beetle. Thirty years later, it's the Volkswagen Golf. In a recent commercial a woman leaves an elegant mews house at the end of a relationship. She discards an expensive fur coat, her pearls, her ring, but not her car keys. She's keeping her Golf! Why? Because it's more reliable than her man.

By being consistent, Volkswagen owns the concept of 'reliability'. It's part of their brand's personality. Consistency is the next guideline. Does the ad help to support the brand's personality, or are we being intentionally inconsistent to change people's attitudes to the brand? Each ad contributes to the consumer's feeling about the brand. If only one ad in a whole campaign differs from the others, then the consumer becomes confused and no longer trusts the brand.

Clients love the word 'unique' and they are right to look for something that discriminates their brand from the competition. Uniqueness rarely exists in the brand itself these days, unless it's of the "with added ZBDX40" nonsense.

Slapping on a label that says "Includes 'Bactoban'" is not enough. The brand itself must communicate in a manner that differentiates it from others. If there isn't a unique brand or product benefit, then the expression of it must be. The ad must become the point of difference.

Let's look at another car example, this time different ads from different agencies, all advertising cars with the same consumer benefit – the roof comes down. They're convertible versions of existing models. One ad shows the sun blazing down on the car and says, "Now with extra headroom, 93 million miles". Another has a similar picture but says, "Now with added vitamin E". The third shows a young fashion designer lounging by the car with the line, "The return of the see-through top". And in today's laddish magazines, you might see something like, "You'd get noticed with your top off". The expressions are striving to be unique, despite the products' similarities.

By now you have one 'big idea', consistency and a differentiating promise. What else do you need?

9.4 INVOLVING THE CONSUMER

Keeping the consumers' questions in mind, the next one a client should ask themselves is, "Does my ad involve my consumer?" It's not enough for an ad just to have impact. Once it's got the consumer's attention, it must generate enough interest for the product benefit to be taken on board and seen as relevant.

Problem/solution ads are very popular with clients because if they've identified the problem correctly, the consumer will become involved enough to listen to their solution.

Involving ads often ask questions. That's why you see so many headlines beginning with "How?", "Where?", "What?", "When?" and "Why?"

An insurance company recently asked, "Does your pension move jobs when you do?" You can bet theirs does, and if you're in their target market you can bet yours doesn't. It couldn't be clearer, which leads us to another question to ask yourself: "Is it simple?", "Is it clear?", "Can the ad be misunderstood?" (Anything that can be will be.) Ambiguity, too many thoughts and inconsistency all add to confusion and confused consumers, and confused customers don't add to your sales. Your ad may be clear, but is it relevant? A client will never involve a consumer if the ad is not relevant.

A headline that says, "A free alarm clock when you join our funeral cover-plan" has its problems, but back to our mobile pension. The benefit differentiates from the static competition, but the way it's expressed is what involves the consumer.

However, something else is going on. A relationship is being established. Relationships develop when people understand each other. The insurance company understands that with an insecure job market, people are concerned about their pension arrangements, but it expresses the concern in a reassuring, colloquial manner. There are other things to consider when assessing whether an ad has a relationship with a consumer.

- Are the people in the ad right?
- Is the setting too aspirational?
- What's the appropriate tone of voice?

How people look, behave and speak are crucial factors in any relationship. When we trust someone, we say they are 'genuine', so ads have to be 'genuine' to gain consumer trust. Ask yourself, "Is it credible?"

This doesn't rule out humour or hyperbole ("93 million miles of head room" is evidence of that). The joke is the means used to sell the vehicles' benefit. Secret ingredient "ZBDX40" is less acceptable.

Yet all this may be in vain if we forget one thing: are the brand name and the idea inseparable? This isn't about making the logo bigger. It's about fusing the brand and the idea together. Try word association with some of your favourite brands.

We know Volkswagen equals reliability, Flora equals health,

Domestos equals peace of mind. That's because the fusion has worked, and of course, because the idea was campaignable.

Campaigns are less prevalent than they once were. One-off, short-term ads dominate many a marketer these days. Even so, checking the campaignability of an idea is a good way of checking its strength.

A recent poster showed a frog on a yellow background. In the top right-hand corner was a small logo and the word 'Rivets'. It wasn't selling frogs, it wasn't selling rivets. The logo was for Yellow Pages and what made you feel good was that they allowed you to make the connection. 'Rivets' is the sound frogs make in jokes, and you can find unusual things like rivets in Yellow Pages. The 'feel good factor' is important to Yellow Pages. It's the keystone of their long-running campaign.

Indesit pride themselves on their uncomplicated electrical goods, so much so that their slogan is 'Simple Ideas Last Longer' – a commandment in itself! A robust idea will suggest executions other than the one put before the client.

SUMMARY

In this chapter we've tried to define an idea. We've judged the creative process and established some criteria for judging creative work. Refer back to Chapter 4 to look at what's involved in producing an advertisement for television, print and radio once the idea has been bought by the client.

Chapter 10
Understanding the Media Marketplace

During the last two decades, the main characteristic of the media marketplace has been its ever growing complexity. The choice available to the consumer has increased beyond recognition. As consumers demand more in all aspects of life, including media, their appetites are satisfied by media owners willing to offer something extra in their own battle for market share. The end result is audience fragmentation. This requires greater media planning skills to understand how and where to influence consumers.

To attempt to explain the media changes in one chapter is ambitious, if not unrealistic. Therefore, we will only begin to scratch the surface of the key changes affecting each medium and their implication on media planning today.

Before thinking about each medium in more detail we should appreciate each medium's share of total advertising. This will give us an understanding of each medium's relative size.

Share of total advertising (1997)	
Press	60.3%
Television	31.3%
Outdoor	4.3%
Radio	3.4%
Cinema	0.7%

Source: Zenith Media

In terms of total size the advertising marketplace in 1997 was worth £13.1 billion (including agency commissions and production costs).

10.1 NATIONAL PRESS

UK national newspapers are a huge medium, read by three quarters of all adults daily. In addition, the UK has over 1,350 regional newspapers comprising morning and evening dailies, Sundays and weeklies. We will only concentrate on national press in this section.

The Audit Bureau of Circulation (ABC) classifies fourteen dailies and eleven Sundays from ten publishers as national UK titles from which we derive the following market shares.

Publisher	Title	Percentage Circulation Share
News International	*Sun, NOTW, Times, Sunday Times*	32.7
Mirror Group	*Mirror, Record, People, Sunday Mirror*	22.6
Associated	*Mail, Mail on Sunday, Evening Standard*	19.4
United News & Media	*Express, Daily Star, Express on Sunday*	11.7
Telegraph	*Daily and Sunday Telegraph*	7.4
Guardian Media Group	*Guardian, Observer*	2.7
Independent Newspapers	*Independent, IOS*	1.5
Financial Times Ltd	*FT*	1.1
Others	*Racing Post, Scotsman, Scotland on Sunday, Sunday Business, Sunday Sport*	0.9

Source: ABC (March-August 1998)

Revenues are attracted by the size of circulation and readership each title commands. For the right product, targeting the right audience, to have the ability to reach 3.7 million adults via one insertion in *The Sun* is an attractive option. At the other end of the spectrum, the 357,000 readers of the *Financial Times* is equally appealing for the right advertiser. Thus, targeting via specific title selection is one of the key benefits of the UK's national press structure. The range of titles from populars (*Sun/Mirror*) through the mid-markets (*Mail/Express*) to the quality broadsheets (*Times/Telegraph/Guardian/Independent*) caters for all tastes. Top advertisers in national press tend to be retailers who use the immediacy of a daily/Sunday read to promote their latest promotional and price offers.

A long-term trend within national press is that total circulation is in decline. Sales fell 13 per cent in the decade 1988-1997. Readership, especially among 15-24 year olds, is in the greatest decline as other media take an increasing share of their time.

In an attempt to counter this trend, newspapers have attempted to increase their value by extending their product offering (more sections, weekend listing magazines), increased the amount of promotions and competitions and at the most extreme, cut cover price. At 10p, the Monday edition of *The Times* will have enticed male sport fans to buy (possibly from its key rival, *The Telegraph*), therefore distorting the size and profile of the aggregate Monday-Saturday data.

It is no surprise that newspaper groups have been keen to diversify. Most have set up electronic Internet versions of their main titles in an attempt to maintain readers who may wish to access their product electronically. To date, most sites have lost money as Internet usage is still very low and impossible to measure (thus it won't appeal to advertisers who demand accountability).

10.2 MAGAZINES

In 1998, the industry directory of newspapers and magazines (BRAD) listed over 2,700 consumer magazine titles in the UK. The number of titles changes continually with launches and closures – there were 344 new titles launched in the first six months of 1998 alone. With so many titles, the marketplace is usually analysed by sector.

Magazine Sector	Percentage Circulation (January-June 1998)
Women's Weeklies	23
Women's Monthlies	18
Teenage	10
Men's Monthlies	10
Television Listings	31
Home Interest	6
Music	2

Magazine Sectors

The strength and weakness of each sector reflects trends in society. Women's weeklies are struggling, as their subject areas appear to diverge from the wants of today's consumer. Lost sales in this sector amount to £1million since 1990. Conversely, home interest titles are booming, helped along by the rash of popular television programmes, such as *Changing Rooms* and *DesRes*. There now is a men's sector as well. Gone are the days when a combination of newspaper supplements and special interest titles were the only means of reaching large numbers of men. This sector continues to grow, led by the high circulation titles of *FHM* and *Loaded*.

Advertising within each sector reflects the editorial content covered. For example, in women's magazines the five key categories are: cosmetics and toiletries, clothing, food, pharmaceutical and mail order, which account for almost 70 per cent of total advertising expenditures. In the television listings titles, mail order, motoring, entertainment, food and finance are the key categories, reflecting the difference in target audience and editorial.

Reader Relationship

The relationship readers have with their magazine is something the media planner must tap into. Our understanding needs to go beyond pure readership figures. The Quality of Readership Survey (QRS) is one piece of research, launched in March 1998, that helps planners understand how long the reader spends reading, the number of times a reader picks up the title and behaviour and attitude. Some key findings are:

- The average consumer magazine is read for 54 minutes compared to 25 minutes for newspaper supplements.

- The average consumer magazine is picked up 5.4 times against a newspaper supplement being picked up 2.6 times.

This type of information, coupled with qualitative research by publishers, will become more important in the future. At the risk of repetition, we need to look beyond the numbers. It is the relationship consumers have with media that will increase their receptiveness to advertisers' messages.

10.3 CINEMA

In the last decade alone, cinema admissions in the UK have increased by 85 per cent, with an estimate that admissions will increase to 156 million by 2000. The arrival of the multiplex – purpose-built sites with more than five screens – has fuelled the growth in cinema admissions. In addition, the exhibitors' efforts to ensure an exciting and pleasant 'cinema experience', coupled with the release of good films, have further contributed to cinema's success.

Across the last five years (1994-1998) the top grossing films at the UK box office have been: Four *Weddings And A Funeral, Batman Forever, Independence Day, The Full Monty* and *Titanic*. The mega release of 1999 has been *Star Wars, Episode I*.

With some 2,700 sites in the UK (multiplexes account for 52 per cent of screens) visiting the cinema is a popular leisure activity, particularly among under-35s. Not only are people visiting the cinema in greater numbers, they are visiting more frequently, with the average number of visits per year rising to 4.0, compared to 2.6 in 1987.

The profile of the cinema-goer is unique in comparison with other media – it is young (68 per cent of admissions are among the 15-34 age group) and upmarket (66 per cent are ABC1, making it more upmaket than BBC2). That said, children and the over-35s are growing audience sectors.

Advantages

From an advertiser's point of view, cinema offers advantages that go beyond these numbers. The impact of the large screen is unrivalled, adding to brand recall, image and identity. Recall studies have shown that on average, a cinema commercial is at least five times more powerful in generating advertising recall than television.

The cinema experience is often a shared one (97 per cent of all cinema-goers go with other people), with commercials being enjoyed as an integral part of the cinema experience. The physical size of the medium makes it a good showcase for creative work, a fact that has not gone unnoticed with creatives in advertising agencies. We can all recall the elaborate one or two minute commercials for drinks, cosmetics and clothing with high production values.

Disadvantages

This is all great news, but is there a downside? Sadly, yes. The total number of cinema admissions in one year is the equivalent to about nine episodes of *Coronation Street*, or ten days of national press circulation. As such, coverage is slow to build. For example, the cover built across a twelve week campaign would read as follows:

Adults	26%
15-24 Adults	55%
15-34 Adults	45%

Similarly, in terms of cost-per-thousand, cinema is more expensive compared with television.

Cinema Airtime

When it comes to buying cinema airtime, there are several ways to do this depending on the campaign's objectives. The route to maximising cover and cost efficiency is via an Audience Guarantee Plan (AGP) that offers advertisers a guaranteed level of admissions for a fixed cost-per-thousand. This buying route is not selective by film or audience in order to maximise the all adult delivery. Selectivity is offered by 'Premiere', which works on the same principle as the AGP but allows advertisers to target more specific audiences than the all adult profile (e.g. 15-24 age group). Total selectivity is offered by two purchase methods: by a film package where an advertiser only buys into a specific film, or purchase on an individual screen basis.

Airtime purchase is made from the two sales contractors: Carlton Screen Advertising, who account for 69 per cent of cinema admissions and sell on behalf of major chains, such as Odean, UCI, Virgin and ABC, and Pearl & Dean who account for 31 per cent of admissions selling on behalf of Showcase, Warner, Cine UK and Apollo.

Despite the increase in home entertainment, with the launch of digital television and the attendant channels and interactive services, cinema should continue to enjoy a good future. The cinema experience is unique and it will be some time before this can be replicated in our own front rooms.

10.4 OUTDOOR ADVERTISING

The outdoor market is split into two sectors: roadside and transport. The former, as the name suggests, covers all roadside panels, and the latter covers railway stations, underground stations, buses, airports, taxis and Advans (posters fixed onto the side of mobile vehicles). A third sector is in the process of emerging which can be captured within the term 'ambient' (advertising on petrol-pumps, at point-of-sale within supermarkets and so on).

Advantages

The total outdoor market was worth £500 million in 1997 (5.6 per cent of total display revenue), with roadside accounting for 60 per cent and transport 40 per cent (ambient is excluded from these figures). It was the fastest growing medium in 1997, showing a 17.4 per cent year on year increase. To understand what is behind the growth, we need to examine the reasons why advertisers use the medium.

The key benefits of outdoor advertising can be summarised as follows:

- **Flexibility**. Outdoor is a broadcast medium reaching mass audiences, but through careful site selection has the ability to narrowcast by targeting certain audiences more specifically. It can be bought by individual site, town, region or nationally.
- **Audiences**. The outdoor audiences are mobile, tend to be lighter ITV viewers and more upmarket than the UK population as a whole.
- **Impact**. The constant on street presence ensures a higher viewing frequency than any other medium. When coupled with the larger poster formats (48s/96s) their impact is hard to deny.
- **PR**. A number of clients use the medium to launch a new idea in a PR-able way, thereby ensuring editorial coverage way beyond the value of space bought.
- **Accountability**. The key research measurement of the outdoor industry is via POSTAR, which uses a complex system of traffic and pedestrian counts coupled with a visibility model to calculate the 'likelihood to see' score (not the 'opportunity to see' which previous models relied on).

In addition to these benefits, individual contractors offer further research incentives which usually form part of the overall negotiation.

Outdoor Market Structure

Before gaining an understanding of the market dynamics, it is necessary to appreciate the market structure, both in terms of size and ownership.

There are approximately 100+ contractors in the UK who own 90,000 sites. However, as with most media, there are a few key players who dominate. In the case of outdoor advertising, the 'Big 5' (The More Group, JC Decaux, Maidens, Mills & Allen and TDI) own 75 per cent of all sites. The remaining 25 per cent are owned by a plethora of smaller, regional contractors, without whom advertisers would not be able to achieve a good geographic spread of sites.

There is a dominance of 6 and 48 sheets within the marketplace. These are two different formats; 6s (1.8m x 1.2m) are a key portrait size dominating the high street, whilst 48s (3.06m x 6.12m) are a key landscape size found on major roads on the edge of and between towns and cities. This major difference in location immediately polarises the audiences they appeal to and the types of advertiser who use them. 6s are often used by FMCG advertisers appealing to housewives, or by the impulse sector appealing to young adults, two audiences that frequent town centres. On the other hand, 48s are more likely to appeal to motorists (due to their siting), and are used for branding to an adult audience.

Over the last few years the outdoor market has seen the consolidation of sizes into 6s, 48s and 96s, which now account for 88 per cent of all revenue. The latest development has been the creation of a premium sector by removing 'poorer sites' to improve audience delivery by increasing illumination on 48s, harmonising posting periods across the key contractors and moving to shorter (usually two week), heavier display periods. This has added a layer of accountability and professionalism that the outdoor industry has lacked in the past.

These developments have resulted in the outdoor medium becoming more attractive to many advertisers. The end result has been that demand has outstripped supply in some months, pushing cost increases ahead of inflation. Ironically, it is the success that the medium has enjoyed of late that may curtail its future growth. The cost of running a heavyweight campaign at certain times of the year is equivalent to running a medium weight television campaign during the cheapest times of the year, and despite the various pieces of research available, there is none that has convinced me that the effect of posters and television are comparable. They work in different ways to persuade and remind consumers, but when it comes to sales effect I have never seen any research on posters to challenge television. The outdoor medium needs to be careful not to price itself out of the market.

10.5 TELEVISION

Television in the UK is the most sophisticated and measured of all media. Minute by minute research is available to tell us who is watching, where and for how long. Data is researched by Audits of Great Britain (AGB) for the Broadcasters' Audience Research Board (BARB).

Viewing habits remain relatively consistent, with the average individual watching 3 hours and 35 minutes of television a day in 1997. An abundance of new channels does not encourage people to watch more. Here, as elsewhere in the world, viewers can only regularly cope with a repertoire of ten to twelve channels.

In this section we will concentrate on the commercial channels ITV, Channels 4 and 5 and satellite.

ITV

ITV is comprised of fifteen regionally based broadcasters who serve fourteen areas of the country (there are two in London) with local and shared network programmes. The one national ITV contract is held by GMTV, who transmits between the hours of 06.00-09.25.

ITV is the largest single UK channel, and as such has had the most to lose as new competitors have entered the television arena. Since 1992, this has emerged in many forms: satellite and cable, an independent Channel 4, Channel 5 and a more competitive BBC1 and BBC2. Since 1992, ITV is estimated to have lost 30 per cent of its audience. However, ITV audiences are still large in comparison to other channels.

ITV Top 10 Programmes (December 1998)

Programme	Audience (in millions)
Celebrity Stars in your Eyes	16.3
Coronation Street	16.0
Heartbeat	14.6
You've been Framed	11.8
Men for Sale	11.5
Emmerdale	11.4
You've been Framed (Christmas special)	11.1
Heartbeat (Christmas special)	10.8
Grafters	10.2
Dennis Norden	10.0

Source: BARB

In response to advertisers' demand for a better performance, ITV has set itself targets for share of viewing in peak: 38 per cent in 1998 and 40 per cent in 2000. Coupled with moving *News at Ten*, this is enough, at least in the short-term, to placate advertisers' calls for increased commercial minutage to ease inflation.

ITV is sold by three sales houses who represent the local regions: Laser sells on behalf of LWT, Granada/Border and Yorkshire/Tyne Tees. Carlton, on behalf of Carlton (London), Central and WCTV and TSMS sells the remainder: Meridian, Anglia, HTV, STV, Grampian and Ulster. Broadly speaking, each sales house controls one third of ITV revenue (the Office of Fair Trading limits the sales houses to 25 per cent of total television revenue).

Channel 4

Channel 4 went on the air in 1982 and was conceived as a 'pure publisher', meaning that all its programmes were either commissioned or bought in. It did not sell its own airtime until 1993 (ITV sold this in return for a levy). It now sells airtime in competition with the rest of commercial television. Most is sold nationally and some by six macro regions: London, South, Midlands, North, Scotland and Ulster (a separate Welsh service, S4C, also exists).

Advertisers use Channel 4 for one very good reason: its audience profile is in line with that of the UK. ITV's is older and more downmarket. Nevertheless, advertisers still attach a premium to the sheer size of ITV audiences, which allows campaigns to build rapid mass coverage. Channel 4 is a complement to ITV, not a substitute.

Channel 4 Top 10 Programmes (December 1998)

Programme	Audience (in millions)
The Quick & The Dead	4.1
Friends	4.0
Countdown	3.7
Barb Wire	3.2
Father Ted (Christmas special)	3.2
The Snowman (film)	3.0
Little Women	3.0
Riverdance/New Show	2.7
Johnny Meets Madonna	2.6
Storm Force	2.6

Source: BARB

Channel 5

Channel 5 is a consortium of media companies (United News and Media, Pearson, CLT and Warburg Pincus) who won the ten-year national licence with a bid of £22 million per year. It started broadcasting on 30 March 1997, having spent some £150 million retuning the videos of the entire population. Compared with ITV, its programme budget is small – some £110 million per annum compared with ITV's £750 million – and as a result its programme content is variable. It currently takes an all adult audience share of 4 per cent and is keeping to its pledge to be 'modern mainstream', attracting a midmarket, younger viewing profile which is useful to advertisers trying to track down 'lighter' commercial television viewers.

Channel 5 Top 10 programmes (December 1998)

Programme	Audience (in millions)
UEFA Cup Football	2.8
Beast of War	1.8
Wharf Rat	1.7
In the Lake...Woods	1.7
Running Wild	1.7
Desperado (film)	1.6
The Real Monty	1.5
Great LA Earthquake	1.5
Sex and Shopping	1.5
When...Cradle Falls	1.5

Source: BARB

Satellite/Cable

UK households can supplement the four or five analogue channels they are able to receive by terretrial transission by subscribing to cable or satellite services. These are supplied by local cable franchises and BSkyB respectively.

At the end of 1997, 6.5 million households (28.5 per cent) subscribed to either cable or satellite. It is expected that 42 per cent of all homes will subscribe by 2005. The growth of satellite and cable over the last ten years has resembled the earlier spread of colour television, VCRs and CDs, as services first confined to early-adopters spread to a genuine mass market. Two key groups of subscribers are young men, who purchase the sport channels, and homes with young children, which subscribe to the children's channels. Satellite penetration of both these groups is among the highest.

Around 60 channels are available to UK viewers, although some are divided into separately branded packages. BSkyB offers a tiered subscription package to dish homes, while cable operators supply various selections to their subscribers.

The advent of new channels has gradually raised the share of viewing time that multi-channel audiences devote to cable and satellite channels. In 1997 cable and satellite television took 38 per cent of viewing in multi-channel homes, a proportion that should rise to over 40 per cent by 2000.

Top 10 Programmes on Satellite/Cable (December 1998)

Programme	Audience (in millions)
World's Worst Drivers	0.3
Super Sunday Live	0.3
Magic:/Revealed	0.3
Police Stop	0.3
Stargate S G-1	0.3
Secret/Beauty/Exposed	0.2
Prickly Heat	0.2
Football Analysis	0.2
When Good Time...Bad	0.2
South Park	0.2

Source: BARB

For media planners, the challenge in television is to ensure the correct channel and programme mix as audiences become increasingly difficult to reach. For the stations, it is to fight for market share by offering better programming and programme promotion. Given the infancy of digital, that challenge is only just beginning.

10.6 RADIO

According to RAJAR (Radio Joint Audience Research), nearly 41 million UK adults (86 per cent of the total) listen to the radio at some time during a week. Of this figure, commercial radio reaches 28.7 million (60 per cent) per week who spend an average of just over two hours per day listening. Over a month, the reach of all adults aged 15+ rises to over 80 per cent.

There are currently 188 commercial radio stations, and the number is expected to rise to over 250 by the year 2000, not including digital radio stations. Airtime is sold by four major sales houses who represent various groups of stations. These are: Capital Advertising, EMAP on air, OPUS and Katz.

Independent Radio (IR) is served by a variety of stations, from the local station reaching 10,000 adults each week to the big city stations reaching millions. There are also three national commercial stations: Classic FM, Virgin am and Talk Radio, plus Atlantic 252, which reaches approximately two thirds of the UK population. Most listeners have the choice of seven or eight commercial stations, four national stations, two local stations, an FM regional station and possibly a smaller community service.

Radio listening peaktime is during the morning. Commercial radio audience peaks at around 8.30 am during weekdays, when 15 per cent of the population are listening. Audiences steadily fall during the day with a brief revival during the afternoon 'drivetime' at around 5.00 pm.

The battle for radio listening share between IR and the BBC has been raging for several years, although currently IR has taken the lead over the BBC. Of the IR share, independent local radio takes the largest portion with 39.9 per cent and the four national commercial stations each take smaller pieces of the remaining 10.1 per cent.

The large variety of different station formats (music, speech, community) and frequency (am/fm) means that audience profiles differ by station. In general, commercial radio is more popular with young listeners: 25-34 year olds spend up to 16.2 hours for listening per week compared with the average 14.7 hours.

Over the last decade, the number of radio services in the UK has doubled, with advertising revenue showing an even greater growth. Revenue reached £393 million in 1997, up 141 per cent from 1990, making radio a 3.4 per cent medium.

The future challenge for radio is for the industry to decide how to make digital profitable for themselves as a business and more interesting for the listeners. Currently there are no compelling reasons for consumers to think about digital.

SUMMARY

More choice means greater opportunity for the advertiser. Taking up the right opportunities will result in competitive advantage. Taking up the wrong ones will cost dearly.

The challenge for advertisers and planners alike is to understand all aspects of the consumers' life and to incorporate new and relevant opportunites into the media solution. For the brave, the future is exciting.

Chapter 11
Media Planning Principles

The development of a coherent and effective media strategy relies on the collective understanding of the main players in the drama: the client whose money is being spent; the media planner/strategist; the creative department; the media owner who will provide the conduit to the target audience and the advertiser who wishes to persuade or influence.

To develop an effective media plan, the advertising, marketing and business objectives all need to be clearly understood before they can be implemented or translated into a media plan. The input of the client and the marketing or product manager is critical. The business objectives and the expected return on investment must be calculated and the scope of the marketing task clearly defined. Advertising, and the role it will play, emanates from all of this shared learning.

Advertising is expected to play a key role in the development of a product or service and this can be predefined. The clearer the objectives, the easier it will be to develop the media plan, which of course will have its own objectives.

Advertising is the most visible, though not necessarily the largest, component of the communications mix in the UK. Some would think it gets a disproportionate level of attention compared to the influence it exerts. Perhaps because of this, creating a clear view of the expectation of the role of advertising is critical.

11.1 ADVERTISING PLANNING

The client has to ensure that the key elements of the advertising planning process must be analysed before the media-planning task is undertaken. The steps in this process can be summarised as follows.

1. Identify the target audience.
2. Determine the advertising objectives.

3. Determine the budget.
4. Develop the media plan.
5. Create the advertising message.
6. Evaluate the effectiveness.

Perhaps the most important of these, as far as the media planner is concerned, is the work done by the marketing department to define the target consumer. As with all marketing decisions, advertising starts with the segmentation of the potential market to identify those key target segments seen as most relevant. As already stated, most advertising attempts to persuade consumers, or potential consumers, that products or services meet their needs or will offer them increased value. The characteristics of the target segment should determine the whole nature of the media plan (when the advertising is shown and the media chosen to display it).

11.2 DEVELOPING THE MEDIA STRATEGY

Who is the Target Consumer?

The heterogeneous market has to be broken down into customer groups that have similar needs. Different customer groups have different expectations and require different types of communications. Hi-fi enthusiasts have different needs than the tone deaf; business people have different travel needs to tourists; speciality manufacturers want different support to commodity builders.

The potentials of the different segments then have to be assessed. Companies have to choose which segment they want to focus on. This will depend on the attractiveness of the segments: their size, growth potential, profitability and competitiveness. From a business perspective, it depends where the company is positioned to develop a competitive advantage. Which segments would most value the company's products and expertise?

Advertising messages and media plans work best when they are in tune with the culture of the target audience, are interesting to them and present a solution to their needs in an interesting way.

Media Research

Research is not a universal panacea to discover the target consumer's needs, wants and habits, but media planning is well served by industry-sponsored research. Each of the main media has their own Joint Industry Committee (JIC) for the maintenance of standards in the areas of research associated with their medium. This provides reassurance about the technical aspects (how many, how often, how detailed and how measured) of the chosen media. This quantifiable aspect of media research into the target audience provides the bedrock of 'the media negotiation/deal' but has no real credibility as a sustainable method of developing the target group on its own.

Demographic Data

Of course, quantitative media research can be supplemented by demographic data available from standard government departments, such as the Central Statistical Office (CSO) or Central Office of Information (COI). This will provide all the data needed on age, class, family size, geography, regionality and occupation.

These two aspects (media data and demographic data) are steps in the right direction to understand the target audience. More and more, however, the real discriminators are the beliefs, attitudes and behaviours that bond groups of individuals into consumer or potential consumer groups.

Target Group Index (TGI)

To develop a clearer understanding of these elements of the consumer, the media planner has a number of research tools at his disposal. The most commonly used is Target Group Index (TGI). This self-completed survey of 25,000 adults is the largest conducted in the UK, and seeks out information on their purchasing habits across a wide spectrum of products and services. This enables us to define consumers beyond demographics by their attitudes and lifestyle ('green consumers'), their media consumption (readers of the *Daily Telegraph*) or product consumption (heavy users of brand 'x'). When this data is cross-tabulated with the wealth of other data on the survey, an accurate picture of who the consumer is, how often they purchase, which medium they watch/listen to and when can be built up. Checked against the client's own data or tested out against customer focus groups, this single source of data provides the planner with an invaluable insight into completing the first stage in any media plan: defining the target audience. Once this stage is completed, the question of how to reach them is the next challenge.

11.3 SELECTING THE MEDIUM

The media choice should be determined by the results of the work already done in defining the target audience and understanding the best creative vehicle able to be used. Before selecting the medium, it is essential that as an advertiser you have a good understanding of the composite of each of the main media types

There has been an explosion in the choice of media available to the consumer in the last twenty years or so, as can be seen in the chart below.

	1980	1998
Television Channels	ITV	ITV, C4, C5, 60+ cable and satellite channels
Radio Stations	26	188
Cinema Screens	1,200	2,700
National Newspapers	16	25
Consumer Magazines	1,624	2,700
Poster Sites	130,000	90,000+

Source: ITC/RAB/BRAD/CAA

All these and a plethora of ambient media choice that ranges from advertising on the back of bus tickets to advertising on local authority fire engines ensures advertising exposure.

Faced with the overwhelming array of choice, the media planner has four key questions to answer before deciding on the most appropriate medium to use. All the questions emanate from an understanding of the disposition of the target audience.

1. **How will the advertising work?**

   Will it be required to convey detailed and significant facts about important issues such as health and safety? Is it designed to entertain and be humourous? Will the advertising work by persuasion, by competitive facts, by repetition of the proposition, by the strength of the product offering, etc.?

2. **Does the product category demand special understanding, is the competitive activity significant, can the creative impact be assessed?**

   The product category may have specific requirements placed on any advertising that may determine the media choice. For example, if the product is in the financial sector, the disclaimers required might mean that in many instances radio may not be suitable. If the product being advertised requires some sort of direct response, press may be deemed more efficient than television. All these and other decisions will be made as objectively as possible and irrespective of the price of each of the media.

   The backdrop to all of these aspects of the media planning process will always be how to get the best from the creative material.

   On the subject of the price of each of the available media, the size of the budget available may be the overriding factor in any discussion of the most appropriate media. To get the best from the media planning process still demands that the questions have to be asked and answered before progress can be made towards creating the media plan.

3. **How often is the media used?**

   The frequency of the availability of any media is of vital importance to the decision-making process. In the FMCG sector, there is little point in using a medium that is best described as infrequent when the main reason for advertising is to launch a product and get a quick uptake by the consumer and the trade. The long-term image and status of a brand can also be undermined by the use of a medium that is characterised by ubiquity. Careful consideration should be given to the way the consumer will be able to access the media.

As well as the medium's frequency of use, the characteristics of each medium also needs to be considered. Is the nature of the medium one of entertainment or information? Is the entertainment seen as leisurely, such a monthly interest magazine, or more of a cursory scan, such as a gossip weekly? Is the information of a transient nature, such as the environment of a chat show, or one of substance, such as a scientific journal? All these questions have to be answered.

4. **What about attention, interest and environment?**

As research into the media habits of the consumer has become more sophisticated, the media planners have challenged the view that an advertising message is equally as good, irrespective of its position. The position in a magazine, the programme break an advertisement appears in or the poster site chosen are all-important considerations, and indeed some media owners are equally convinced of this.

It should be clearly understood that the plethora of research that has been developed around the quality of the advertising message and the media is part of the buying and selling process. There are vested interests by media owners to use research to support the proposition of the unique value of their share of any medium. The smart media planners know this and use their experience to disseminate the information available. Media planning is about making informed choices.

The work undertaken on attention values, viewer loyalty, programme appreciation, topic interest, specially chosen to read or watch all have to be investigated and prioritised to help create the most effective media plan. Prompting the desired response is the number one challenge for the media planner.

11.4 WHAT PROMPTS A RESPONSE?

We have discussed the advertising objectives and the advertising strategy. Two fundamental questions are how many people do we need to reach with the advertising, and once that has been decided, how many times does the target audience need to see our advertising?

We are now entering the realm of 'coverage and frequency'. The 'how often and when' is at the heart of the media plan. Establishing the timing of the activity and the weight (the coverage and frequency over time) is critical. The key areas that need to be discussed before the appropriate coverage and frequency objectives can be set can be summarised as follows.

1. **The category and the product.**

    Will my advertising take place in a highly competitive environment and is the product one that will be a frequent purchase, such as a washing powder, or in the luxury sector, such as a car? Whichever it is, the timing of the advertising will be different.

2. **The proposition.**

    What will I be saying in my advertising? Is it a simple message, such as 'sale starts today' or something much more complicated, such as a financial product (e.g. an ISA)? Obviously, questions of this nature are part of the advertising planning and, whilst the media planner can give advice, the decision will need to be a shared one with the advertiser when all of the marketing variables are assessed.

3. **Creative content.**

    Does the advertising demand a quick response? Does the product have a short shelf life? Is the advertising dependent on a style that is reliant on humour? Will the consumer get the joke and be quickly bored? Will I need more than one piece of copy? Do I need to show ads in a particular order? Are they in any sense time or date sensitive? All these questions and the subsequent answers will help structure the media plan. Armed with all this information, how does the media planner put together the plan that will help me sell more products?

Television Rating Point

Even more decisions have to be made. Armed with some basic units of media currency, we can construct a plan in a number of ways subject to the answers we decided on in the question above. Let us take the example of a television plan.

100 TVRs can be put together as follows.

PLAN 1	100 TVRs	10 weeks activity	10 per cent of the potential audience seeing the advertising ten times.
PLAN 2	100TVRS	3 days activity	50 per cent of the potential audience seeing the advertising twice.

From the above examples we can see that the equation

$$Coverage \times Frequency = TVRs.$$

All that is fine, but there is significantly more to the construction of the ideal media plan than the absolute numbers of TVRs. The questions of which channels I should choose and the programmes I should be in still have to be decided.

It is possible to take the two plans outlined above and use programmes as follows.

PLAN 1	One programme such as the evening news getting ten TVRs that we can use ten times.
PLAN 2	One episode of *Coronation Street* getting 33 TVRs that we can use three times.

The weight of advertising and the programmes chosen will thus determine the structure of the media plan.

11.5 COVERAGE

When we are thinking about a media plan and we have decided how many people we want our advertising to reach, we have a number of choices to make the best use of that plan as far as the timing of activity goes. Key variables that will change the shape of any media plan and the subsequent response will be drawn from the list below, which is not meant to be exhaustive but is a rough guide to the process.

- New products or launches may require a mass-market approach and the total audience may extend beyond existing users.

- Existing products may be searching for new users by brand development and seek the new users in a new or smaller segment of the market than is usually advertised to.

- High-interest categories may demand an intensive bout of activity against the whole of the target audience.

- Products that have a low purchase frequent usually demand a high level of intrusion against the target group. This is an area where restricting the scope of the advertising can lead to lost opportunities.

- Advertising that demands a high level of creative impact for its success is usually part of an explosive style of media campaign planning where as many people as is possible see the advertising to ensure that the talked-about aspect of the campaign will give it longevity and fame.

All of the above advertising and media campaign scenarios are bonded by the need to concentrate the activity of their advertising and to reach the chosen target audience in a narrow time band. This type of campaign is typically called a 'burst' and in the broadcast media it will last from four to six weeks. In the print media the time can vary, but will typically last over a ten to fourteen day period. American terminology brands this type of activity as a 'flight'. The alternative approach to all of the above is to drip the advertising through the campaign period.

11.6 FREQUENCY

Deciding on the length of an advertising campaign, who it should reach and how long it should last is the first part of the media plan equation that will hopefully lead to more market sales and share.

To make best use of the advertising budget we have to be able to work out how many times the target audience should see the advertising. This aspect of the media, planning process, known as 'frequency', is arguably the most intangible of all the elements of media planning.

The "what is effective frequency" debate got up a head of steam when the conventional wisdom of "once to see, once to remind and once to buy" school of media planning lost momentum in the 1980s.

The truth of the matter is that, despite the fading belief in this conventional wisdom, there were many changes in the choice of media available and the way the media was presented. There was an inevitability that the way media plans were being constructed would need to respond to those changes. Whatever the scientific reasons put forward in the effective frequency debate as to why certain levels are better than others, the zealousness and self-interest of the disciples of various schools of thought can sometimes obscure the basics.

The decision about effective frequency can and still should be prefaced by the answers to some simple questions. Here the skill of the media planner is in knowing the right questions to ask that come from a full understanding of the product and the marketing plan.

- Is the advertising designed to support an existing product, and if so, what are the basic parameters? Is it a frequent purchase? Does the consumer see the product as part of a regular shop?
- Is the product in a highly developed and very competitive sector? Will my advertising prompt others to promote and advertise?
- Is the product a high or low interest category? Does the message need to be driven home or will it be easily assimilated?
- Will advertising frequency effect rate of sale?

Once these and other questions of a similar nature have been answered, the debate about which school of effective frequency should be followed can be resumed. Ideally the media planner will have access to as much data as is possible, and with client input it should be possible to model what the appropriate plan is. This will be based on a range of data normally associated with econometric modelling, but with the additional advantage of media data overlaid to reflect the reality of the dynamic and real market that is the media marketplace.

The conundrum of effective frequency planning may never be answered with real conviction and there is no sure-fire method of ascribing a number to each and every media plan. As long as all the appropriate questions are asked, whether or not the effective frequency is three or some other number, the media plan will be working in the best interest of the client.

The media planner's task is a cross between art and science, but experience and judgement need to be used in equal proportion. Data management will be the main tool in applying some science to the media plan.

"How many" and "how often" are difficult questions to answer, and as previously mentioned are the key questions to be answered in the construction of the media plan. Coverage and frequency decided, the next key area to be considered demands equal attention.

11.7 WHERE DO I ADVERTISE?

Decisions about where to advertise will be determined by many things. The size and ambitions of the brand will govern the regionality of an advertising campaign, and in some cases the budget. Before discussions are made about budget, it is worth looking at the range of options available.

1. Should the advertising concentrate on the areas of sales strength or on sales potential? Is the plan one that is expansionary, or is the role of advertising defensive?
2. Does the plan seek to maximise market strengths or take the opportunistic approach to growing market-share?
3. Will my advertising act as a major influence on the trade in the form of increasing distribution?
4. Is the size of the region or regions to be chosen compatible with the product supply?
5. Has the media plan considered competitive activity and the suitability of the promotional plan for the chosen region?
6. Is the chosen target audience readily available in the area chosen?
7. Is there a demand for the product or is the advertising creating a new market?

Once these questions are answered to a degree of satisfaction, we are closer to completing the plan and understanding the mechanics of the media planning process.

There will always be an opportunity cost of deciding on any of the options that are listed above. Though we have discussed the media planning process as an academic exercise, and there has to be a disciplined approach to reviewing the options available, perhaps the key determinant of how the media plan looks will be the budget.

Earlier in this chapter we spoke of the media plan being task-led, in the sense that the most appropriate logic would be to define the objectives of the advertising and the marketing and then decide on a plan that best meets them. Yet a short stay in the real world quickly leads the media planner to understand that the budget may be finite. What a set budget can buy then takes on real importance for the advertiser and becomes the real driver of the media plan.

11.8 WHAT DOES AN ADVERTISING CAMPAIGN COST?

The following table should be a useful guide not just to the cost, but also to the duration, coverage and the frequency of the advertising campaign.

Medium	Unit	National Campaign	Cost	Adult Cover /Frequency
Television	30"	400 TVRs	£750,000-£1.1 million	82% @ 4.9
National Press	25 x 4 Mono	2 inserts	£220,000	70% @ 3.0
Women's Magazines	Colour	3 months	£250, 000	60% @ 4.0
Radio	30"	4 weeks	£300,000	60% @ 8.0
Cinema	30"	8 weeks	£550,000	18% @ 2.0
Outdoor	6 sheets 48 sheets	2 weeks 2 weeks	£450,000 £440,000	60% @ 15.0 42% @ 11.0

This table will not be the universal panacea to costing a media plan, but should be a useful guide to the basic costs. What the table will show is the range of performance differences in the various media and the range of costs associated with media types. The actual price paid will always be a function of the availability of the media as well as the commitment of the advertiser and the skill of the media planner to present an effective case to the media owner and then the media negotiator to get the best prices.

At this stage, the "how many, how often, where and how much" questions will all have been asked and hopefully been answered. The plan will be presented and needs to be assessed.

11.9 DO I HAVE THE RIGHT PLAN?

Follow this checklist of inclusions and the right plan should become self-evident.

1. Are my communication objectives at the forefront of the thinking in the plan?
2. Are the right people being targeted? Am I going to reach the right people?
3. Will the media chosen give the creative work the best opportunity to promote my product? Conversely, is the creative choice costing me the opportunity for media effectiveness?
4. Do I have the right weight of media? Will my advertising be seen the right number of times?
5. Is the timing of the plan right? Will the plan work with distribution, promotions and trade activity?
6. Do I have the right number of creatives working on the plan? Do I have enough copy to rotate if it's a radio campaign? Will the typeface be big enough for a poster site? Have I used all the opportunities to test the creative in the media before I spend the budget?
7. Has the plan looked at the effect that any competitive activity may have on my media plan?
8. Have I chosen the right areas to advertise in?

9. Finally, if I gave my media department an extra 10 per cent to spend, what difference would it make? Would I lose that much if I had to cut the budget by the same 10 per cent?

Should that be the end of it then? Media is not a precise science and you should be able to apply some of the following invaluable qualities to decide if the media plan is right.

- Subjective judgement.
- Experience.
- Case histories from the product category and media type.
- Common sense.

Media will be a significant proportion of the marketing budget. Give it the time it deserves, involve yourself in the process and get the best for your brand. Understanding the media planning process will not explain the alchemy that sometimes passes for media planning, but it will prompt the right questions.

GLOSSARY

Developing creative and media plans is becoming an increasingly sophisticated business. The technical language associated with this discipline has increased apace.

From the relatively tranquil media world of the 1950s with one commercial television station and no commercial radio, we have moved to an era of regulation and media and advertising opportunities that proliferate by the day. These opportunities have created a language that acts as a facilitator for the business of media, yet can also act as an obstruction to clear-minded and relevant decision-making.

In preparing this glossary, I am mindful that the reader will have questions about words and terms that are constantly used in the advertising business. Media planning and buying and all points that emanate from it should be a means of helping clients sell products or services and contribute to the success of the marketing effort.

If you are unable to find the answer to your question in this glossary, please follow one invaluable piece of advice – just ask and if at first you don't understand, ask and ask again. You have the right to a clear, concise answer.

A

ABC — Audit Bureau of Circulation. An independent body responsible for auditing the circulation figures of paid for magazines and newspapers. Publishers are not obliged to submit to audit, but most do. This is to ensure that media planners and buyers accept the circulation figures as fact and can form the basis of meaningful negotiation for advertising space.

AGB — Audits of Great Britain. A market research company that undertakes fieldwork and processes research results. Currently has the contract for processing all television audience measurement.

AGP — Audience guarantee plan. An agreed media plan that specifies how many consumers will be reached with an advertising message.

AIR — Average issue readership. The term used to estimate the number of people who claim to have read or looked at one or more issues of a specific publication in a specific research period. The usual source of information relating to readership is the National Readership Survey (NRS).

AIRC — Association of Independent Radio Contractors. A trade organisation representing the radio industry on issues relating to legislation and regulation of the industry.

AM — Amplitude modulation. A radio waveband carrying a signal on a fixed frequency, such as 909AM, but has variable quality of sound. An AM radio station broadcasts in mono sound only.

A/S ratio	Advertising to sales ratio. A method of setting advertising budgets based on an actual or hypothetical relationship between sales and the investment in media and marketing.
ASA	Advertising Standards Authority. An industry watchdog responsible for investigating complaints from the general public if advertisements are deemed not to conform to the code of being legal, decent, honest and truthful.
adstock	A term that has its origin in market modelling and the discipline of econometrics. Essentially a statement of the total number of people who are influenced by an advertising campaign and how many of those people are likely to be influenced in any new campaign by what those individuals saw or heard in the initial campaign. Often this is stated in the form of a constant proportion of television rating points.
advertising awareness	Data that is gathered by research to gauge if an advertising message has been communicated.
advertising recall	A measure of what content of an advertisement is remembered. This can be music, message, personalities, etc.
advertorial	A hybrid of advertising and editorial, found mainly in magazines. The advertiser is paying for the editorial team to produce a feature endorsing their product in the style of the publication. The main intention is to have the product or service take on the values of the particular publication.
agent	A person, acting on behalf of an advertiser, who will provide services such as creative work, account planning, media planning and buying. Most agents have the legal status and financial responsibility of the principal in law pertaining to contractual issues.

airdate	The first date of the commencement of a television campaign.
ambient	Term used to describe the range of non-traditional forms of out of home media advertising, ranging from postcards to bus tickets, till receipts to supermarket floors, etc.
audience	The designated group to focus the advertising on.
average frequency	The average number of claimed opportunities to see/hear the ads in a schedule among those in the target population who have at least one opportunity to see/hear. This enables the media planner to estimate how often an individual will see an advertisement during a campaign. For example, a campaign that reaches 70 per cent of the target an average of four times means that some will see it more and some less. It is possible to estimate reach at a specified frequency level by means of computer modelling.
average listening hours	Average time spent listening to a radio station per listener. This is defined by taking all the hours listened to an individual station in a week and dividing it by the total number of listeners.
average OTS/OTH	A term used interchangeably with 'average frequency'. Opportunity to see (OTS) refers to print/visual media, opportunity to hear (OTH) to radio.
awareness	A measurement of knowledge of the existence of a brand or its advertising. Can be measured spontaneously (e.g. "Which brands of bottled beer can you think of?") or prompted (e.g. "Which of these have you heard of?").

B

BACC — Broadcast Advertising Clearance Centre.

BARB — Broadcasters Audience Research Bureau Ltd. Responsible for research and measurement of television audiences. The company represents major UK broadcasters: the BBC, Independent Television Association (ITA) and the Institute of Practioners in Advertising (IPA).

BDI — Brand Development Index. A comparative measure of the value of a brand's sales in one market compared with other markets.

BRAD — British Rate and Data. The bible of information on all advertising data in all media. Contents include circulation, cover prices, copy dates and mechanical data required by printers.

BRMB — British Market Research Bureau. Known for producing the TGI survey.

band on — Term used to describe a magazine added to another and given away as part of the package to enhance value.

banner — Space on a web page that is reserved for advertising. Typically a rectangular strip at the top of the page and animated to encourage the surfer to click the image and proceed to a specific page of interest. Counting these 'clicks' electronically is a means of measuring Internet page traffic.

barter — A trading of advertising space and time in return for specific merchandise. Typically used in America and where programmes are traded for advertising space and used in weak economy areas as a means of developing markets.

billboard	American term for outdoor poster, usually of the large landscape variety.
billings	A means of expressing an advertising agency's turnover in terms of the media expenditure it handles.
bleed	An advertisement in which the printed matter runs off the edge of the page of a magazine or newspaper.
body copy	Main text in a press advertisment.
bookmark	Internet term associated with referencing specific pages for regular use.
brand essence statement	Conceptual way of breaking down the elements that contribute to a brand's make up.
brand goodwill scores	Research which indicates how favourably disposed consumers are to your brand.
brand positioning statement	Document that states the fundamentals of the brand, the target audience and the market in which it operates.
break	Advertising time between programmes, or between segments of specific programmes.
break bumpers	A term associated with sponsorship, where short identification spots are used prior to or after commercial breaks in the programme sponsored. Television companies use this format for programme promotions.
brief	Document that starts the creative development process.
broadband cable	Cable with the capacity to carry more than 30 television channels. Also known as wideband cable.

broadsheet Large newspaper format as opposed to tabloid. In the UK market, broadsheet is associated with 'upmarket' press.

browser A programme that allows Internet users to view sites in an 'unscrambled' form. Typical browsers are Netscape Navigator and Microsoft Explorer.

burst Advertising campaign concentrated into short periods of time to get as much attention as is possible in a short period of time. The opposite term is 'drip campaign' (*see also drip, continuity, flight, laydown, pulsing, strike rate*).

buttons Small clickable shapes on an Internet page designed to take the browser to the advertiser's page.

buying brief A set of objectives agreed with clients to ensure that expected results are achieved. In television this would be expected to include target audience and programmes and channels to be used.

C

CA — Cable Authority. Regulatory body of the cable industry, responsible for authorising cable authorities and public authorities to install cable services and then regulates those services.

CAA — Cinema Advertising Association. The trade association of cinema advertising contractors established in 1953. Its main purpose is to maintain standards in cinema advertising.

CACI — An information and marketing services company. Developed the Acorn system of geo-demographic targeting commonly used in direct mail.

CAVIAR — Cinema and Video Industry Audience Research. Provides information on cinema attendance and profiles of audience for adults and children from the age of seven.

CD-ROM — Compact disc read only memory. Optical storage technology that uses compact discs. Originally used for storage of data, but now has multimedia applications.

CPH — Cost per hundred. The cost of 100 ratings against a specific audience. Used principally (but not exclusively) with reference to television.

CPT — Cost per thousand. The cost of achieving 1,000 impressions against a specific target audience. Total cost of the campaign divided by the total gross impressions.

cable penetration — The total number of homes in a cable provider's area that are capable of receiving the cable service of television programmes, phone and computer services.

Glossary

cable TV — Television distribution service for terrestrial, satellite and cable-only services.

campaign — The entire process and duration of the advertising effort.

cancellation period — The time after which it is not possible to cancel an advertising campaign without incurring significant penalties from media owners. The time-frame varies, as does the size of the penalty. As with most things in the media world, penalties are negotiable.

churn — Term relating to the number of households who take up cable and or satellite but do not renew subscriptions.

circulation — The number of copies of a publication that are circulated, either paid for or free. The most reliable figures are those that are independently audited.

classified — Advertising space within the print media sold by word or line. Usually associated with the sale of goods or services, either commercial or private.

click — The touch of the left side of the mouse by a computer user registering on an advertising space on an Internet web page. Counting clicks gives an advertiser an estimate of the number of individuals that have looked at or passed his page.

cluster group — A collection of individuals with similar attitudes, lifestyles or other defining attributes, grouped together to more accurately define the group that an advertiser wants to target.

clutter — A media environment where there are too many advertisements for reasonable standout and neither the advertiser nor the consumer benefits. Good media planning and negotiation can avoid this.

commercial minutage The number of minutes on television during which commercials may be broadcast. The Independent Television Commission regulates this.

communication mix statement Document that outlines and prioritises the communication channels to be used.

competitive advantage An element of the brand or its postioning that provides a distinct positioning in the eyes of the consumer.

consolidated ratings The number of television ratings recorded from both live and recorded viewing within a week of transmission. Measuring in this way gives an advertiser the opportunity to have an accurate estimate of the number of people who have seen his commercial.

controlled circulation The measured distribution of a publication issued free of charge to readers who qualify under a certain set or criteria, such as professional associations.

co-op advertising Advertising that is paid for by both manufacture and retailer, or by a combination of retailers.

copy The finished advertisement. Includes artwork, film, scripts, etc. Copy deadline is the time at which the advertisements need to be with the media owners to ensure accurate reproduction.

cost rank A method of ranking advertisement vehicles by cost and the number of people they are likely to reach. For example, this enables a quick assessment of the cost efficiency of a proposed magazine schedule. Should not be used as the sole arbiter of effectiveness.

cover mount A free gift attached to the front of a magazine to boost circulation. Typical items are CDs.

cover position Advertisements on the cover of a publication. These can be sold at a premium price and include inside front (IFC) inside back (IBC) or outside back (OBC). The stand-alone nature of the position ensures these positions are in heavy demand.

creative brief Agency interpretation of the client brief with which the creative team is briefed.

cross tracks Poster sites situated across the track at a railway or Underground station, making use of the 'captive audience' theory of marketing.

D

DBS — Direct Broadcast Satellite. Term used to describe a high power satellite broadcast direct to viewer's homes rather than through a cable system.

DDS — Donovan Data Systems. Computer bureau used by advertisers, agencies and media owners. Used as a booking, logging and invoicing system as well as to access research, such as NRS, MMS and similar data.

DMU — Decision-making unit.

DPS — Double page spread. An advertisement printed on two facing pages in a newspaper or magazine.

DRTV — Direct response television. A commercial which carries a call to respond, usually by telephone. Slow to take off in the UK, it is an integral part of many American commercials.

DTH — Direct to home. Satellite transmission received via a dish ariel.

daypart — A section of the viewing or listening day, used to describe the time when groups of individuals are most likely to watch or listen. Additionally, it is used by the sellers of media time to structure rate cards. Typically, the most sought after time of the day on television (such as 21.00-23.00) costs more than other times. On radio the premium time is around breakfast.

decay — Term used to describe the erosion of an advertising campaign's effect over a period of time.

demographics — Standard means of defining a target audience by means of sex, age and socio-economic class. Currently the subject of a major overhaul by the government.

digital television	The transmission of television signals and data as computer digits. Digital television makes use of the existing bandwidths, and by compressing signals is able to offer many more channels than the existing analogue system. Apart from increasing choice there is the opportunity to offer a range of services, such as online banking, electronic games and Internet access to name a few. Finally, in addition to the increased choice, there will be enhanced picture quality and sound.
direct mail	Method used to reach identified prospects and existing customers through personally addressed and customised advertising and promotions.
direct marketing	Techniques which interface directly with the consumer, e.g. direct mail.
direct response advertising	Advertising designed to get potential customers to respond by clipping coupons, telephone response, etc.
display advertising	Used to describe advertising sold in fractions of a page.
domain name	The unique registered named address of a website, such as 'manuted.com'.
drip campaign	Advertising activity that prioritises time advertised over weight. The belief is that it is better to constantly remind rather than 'burst' activity.
drive-time	The most popular and demanded time for radio advertising because it covers the morning and evening commuter periods.
duplication	The number of people who see an advertisement more than once across a number of media vehicles. Also applies to two or more advertisements being displayed in the same location.

E

EIU — Economist Intelligence Unit.

EPOS — Electronic point of sale.

econometric modelling — Computer-based programme developed as a predictive tool.

effective frequency — An established theory about the effect of advertising which claims that consumers need to see an advertisement several times before it prompts action. Precisely what the effective reach of a particular commercial is remains a source of continued debate.

encrypted — Used to describe a television channel whose signal is scrambled to ensure only those who have subscribed can view.

establishment survey — An annual survey carried out to provide the basis of BARB recruitment.

F

FM (print) — Position in a magazine or newspaper facing matter, such as editorial content rather than another advertisement. This is a preferred position when buying many print campaigns.

FMCG — Fast-moving consumer goods.

flight — A period of consecutive days or weeks of advertising within an overall campaign.

fly posting — Posters displayed illegally on either private or public property. Used by record companies and a range of urban activists.

footprint — The geographical coverage area of a satellite transponder.

48 sheet — Large landscaped poster site 10' high by 20' long. Usually located in areas of high traffic density.

The geographical coverage area of a satellite transponder.

four plus — A term in measuring television campaigns that describes that part of the target group that have had four or more exposures to one ad.

fragmentation — The audience that is increasingly difficult to reach because of increased media choice.

front weight — A campaign will be described as 'front weighted' when there is more activity planned at the beginning of the run rather than the end.

G

GMTV Good Morning Television.

GRP Gross rating point. A measure of the total audience exposure of a campaign. GRPs are expressed as a percentage of the target audience population.

gatefold A press advertisement that folds out. Gives an advertiser a minimum of two pages of continuous space. Often attached to the front inside cover of a magazine.

geodemographic targeting Technique to reach consumers depending on the type of housing and residential area in which they live.

gross A descriptor for terms, such as audience, impacts and reach. Conveys the idea of totality, including all 'overlap'. All gross measures within the same media can be added together to provide a total for the media campaign.

gutter The inside page margins where a publication is bound.

H

HTML Hypertext mark-up language. This is an Internet programming language used for creating web pages. It allows for the presentation of information that contains links to related files.

HTV Harlech Television.

hits A hit on the web is a single file request by a user, recorded automatically by the log file on the site's web server.

home page The first page on a website that acts as the starting point for navigation. Home pages link visitors to other pages within the site.

homes passed Homes that could be connected to a cable network because the feeder cable is nearby.

horizontal publication A publication with editorial content and audience appeal that is broad enough to span a wide range of demographics.

I

ILR   Independent Local Radio. A general term referring to commercial radio across the country and controlled by the Radio Authority.

IPA   Institue of Practitioners in Advertising. A body representing the collective views of agencies, liasing with government departments, industry and consumer organisations.

ISBA   Incorporated Society of British Advertisers. Protects and promotes the views and interests of advertisers.

ISP   Internet service provider. A company that provides access to the Internet. Likely to be a company that has a interest in e-commerce.

ITC   Independent Television Commission.

ITV   Independent Television Corporation.

impacts   A term used as an alternative to contacts, impressions and messages.

impressions   A claimed seeing or hearing of an advertisement. The same individual can accumulate more than one impression. Impressions can be added together to give a total for an advertising campaign. For example, if a campaign totals over 20 million impressions, the number of adults who see the campaign is varied and the number of times they see the advertisement can also vary. However, the total is still 20 million impressions.

in charge   The day from which the advertiser starts to pay for sites in a poster campaign.

infomercials   An advertisement on television in the style of an information service or bulletin.

in/on pack offers	Sales promotion technique that usually provides an attractive offer, which can be attached to or placed in the packaging.
integrated communication	Consistent approach to communication tools to ensure that there is a synergy between them.
interactive media	Media with which the consumer/viewer can communicate.
interactive television	Digital development that enables the viewer to take part in programmes.
Internet	The Internet is a system of linked computer networks. Each computer network can connect with others, thus extending the scope and the power. Originally designed by the US Defence Department in 1968.
island site	A press advertisement surrounded by editorial.

J/K/L

JICREG Joint Industry Committee for Regional Press research. Provides a means of quantifying readership across the majority of regional press titles.

job bag Internal agency file that containes all of the relevant documentation on the progress and billing of an advertisement during production.

juxtaposition Posters for competing brands that appear next to one another, either horizontally or vertically, and which are visible simultaneously.

LWT London Weekend Television.

landscape Format for a press ad or a poster that is wider than it is deep.

laydown Pattern of scheduling advertising activity over the period of time of the campaign period.

lifestyle A way of classifying the population by means of their beliefs, activities, possessions, etc., as opposed to socio-economic grades.

line by line The buying of space on an individual site basis in accordance with specific requirements.

live ratings Television ratings that count only the real-time viewing at the time of transmission, as opposed to consolidated ratings.

loading Rate card premiums determined by position and status.

loyalty schemes Sales promotion technique to ensure that consumers continue to buy a brand.

M

MOPS — Mail order protection scheme.

malre-demption — The use of coupons to provide a discount when the product on the coupon is not purchased.

marketing concept — The entire marketing process to profitably optimise a brand's performance.

master mechanical — Artwork for a press advertisement.

media agency — Specialist media services company.

media plan — A summary of the communication objectives that describes the means of achieving them via the advertising vehicle. A plan will consist of marketing, advertising and media objectives, from which a relevant media strategy is devised.

media vehicle — Any advertisement-carrying medium, such as television stations, magazines, poster sites, etc.

merchandising — Additional printed support material, e.g. leaflets, shelf markers, etc.

mono — Black and white ads.

mood boards — Collection of visual elements that demonstrate a facet of a brand, consumer, etc.

mosaic — A geo-demographic planning system whereby residential households and lifestyles are classified by demographic, housing, financial, and census statistics. Groups can be segmented to post code level.

multi-link purchases — Sales promotion technique that links the purchase of different products or brands to promote trial, i.e. buy x and get y free.

N/O

NPA — Newspaper Publishers Association. A body formed by national newspapers that negotiates and is responsible for the agency credit recognition system and the Mail Order Protection System (MOPS).

NRS — National Readership Survey. A comprehensive and extensive readership survey that provides reach and frequency information by age, class, sex and area for over 250 magazines and newspapers.

net homes — Total number of homes in ITV region, excluding any overlap areas.

network centre — The ITV programming and marketing centre.

96 sheet — Landscape poster site measuring approximately 12m x 3m.

OAA — Outdoor Advertising Association. Membership consists of the main poster contractors.

OBC — Outside back cover. Regarded as a premium advertising position in a magazine.

OTH — Opportunity to hear. The number of claimed opportunities to hear an ad amongst the target audience when using a radio.

OTS — Opportunity to see. The number of claimed opportunities to see an ad when using a visual media.

on the run — Colour printed simultaneously with the black and white section of a newspaper or a magazine.

online advertising — Advertising on the Internet. Banner sites are one example.

optimisation	A method of schedule building by computer, by which an optimum is produced to the parameters set by the media planner.
out of charge	The date on which an advertiser ceases to pay for a poster campaign display.
outside repro house	Printer responsible for the reproduction quality of a press ad.
overlap	Multiple counting of individuals who are included in more than one market area, e.g. homes where the reception of one television overlaps with another.
overshow	Posters left on-site after an advertiser has ceased to pay for them.

P/Q

PPA — Periodical Publishers Association. Membership comprises all types of magazine and periodicals.

PSA — Pure station average price. Usually stated as a cost per thousand per month. Easily calculated by dividing the impacts of a specific audience in the given month by contractor advertising revenue. 'Pure' denotes that the revenue is net of volume discounts rebated to the advertiser but before agency commission is paid.

pagination — Volume of advertising specified in terms of pages.

pass on — Readers of a publication other than the purchaser of a specific readership title.

pay per view — Pay television system which allows viewers to purchase an individual television event as opposed to subscription for a whole channel or group of channels.

penetration — The percentage of the population a given medium is available to.

people meters — An electronic device which allows for the measurement of television viewing. This system requires that the individuals in the home record their viewing habits.

pitch — The process whereby competing agencies present strategic or creative ideas to secure an advertising account.

positioning — Where an advertisement is due to appear. This can be specified to narrow or broad tolerance, e.g. inside front cover, first in break, run of paper, etc.

POSTAR	An audience-led research system for the outdoor medium. Panel locations, traffic and visibility are taken into account.
posting	A set time-frame for the posting of all sites in a poster campaign.
pre-empt	A system of buying television airtime in an auction. Under this system airtime can be sold at any one of a number of quoted rates for a given commercial break or segment. The buyers can elect any price but may lose the spot to a buyer willing to pay more for the spot. The theory behind this system is that final cost will be governed by demand. A system not commonly used now that airtime is effectively optimised by the contractor to ensure optimisation of revenue and deliver a fixed price.
premium	A ratecard surcharge for highly demanded positions.
pre-print colour	Colour printed prior to the main publication and fed into the publication when the print run takes place.
primary readership	The purchasers/readers of a publication who are likely to show a greater interest in the publication than that of a pass on reader.
prime time	The hours when television viewing is at its peak, usually in the evening.
profile	Refers to the composition of the audience to a specific media vehicle, showing the percentage of the total accounted for by each sub-demographic.
psychographics	A refinement on demographics, whereby personality and social values are measured and used to classify people.
public relations	Discipline that manages non-paid for publicity, i.e. editorial news bulletins, etc.

pulsing A method of constructing an advertising campaign that calls for an on/off technique augmented by bursts of heavy activity.

push A method where companies provide Internet users with the software they can use to have information delivered directly to them or pushed over the Internet to the PC.

QRS Quality Readership Survey. Research that gives in-depth information on how consumers use and remember elements of a publication.

quintile analysis A method of subdividing a target audience into five equal groups based on their weight of television viewing.

quota sampling A research sampling technique in which researchers interview a pre-set quota of interviewees with given target characteristics. An alternative to a random sample.

R

RAB — Radio Advertising Bureau. The marketing arm of the AIRC.

RAJAR — Radio Joint Audience Research. BBC/Independent joint radio measurement systsem.

ratecard — A price list issued by media owners for different space sizes or time lengths. Described as a statement of the media owner's revenue potential rather than a realistic measure of what they expect to receive for space or time. A starting point for a negotiation.

reach — Percentage of a defined target audience who have the opportunity to see or hear an advertisement during a specified time period.

readers per copy — Readers per copy is calculated by dividing the number of readers by the number of copies bought or circulated.

reading/noting — A research technique in which a sample of readers are asked which advertisements and which parts of those ads they remember and can recall.

recency planning — A theory on the effectiveness of advertising that claims one exposure of the advertising message is enough to produce a sales response, provided it is sufficiently near the time of purchase. Developed by John Philip Jones, the practical manifestation of this theory is that continuity is more effective than burst advertising.

reception — Repeated exposures of an advertisement or a campaign to an audience. It is assumed that several exposures will be needed for a campaign to be determined as effective.

repeat fees   Payments to actors, musicians, etc. who take part in a television commercial. This is related to a basic studio fee and payments vary depending on the exposure the commercial has.

roadblock   A term for placing television spots at the same time on different channels in the same market. Used to block competition and also to maximise the available audience to view a particular commercial.

run of paper   An advertisement booked as run of paper can be positioned at the media owners discretion, anywhere in the publication. Usually the cheapest form of advertising space.

S

SCA	Sustainable competitive advantage. A unique facet of your brand that has long-term potential.
SCC	Single column centimetre. Display advertising in newspapers is usually sold in multiples of this unit.
SOM	Share of market.
STV	Scottish Television.
sales house	An organisation that sells advertising space on behalf of media owners. Also known as sales representatives.
sales promotion	Range of techniques that help add value to a brand and provide a temporary sales boost.
sampling	The technique of selecting a representative subgroup of a specified population from whom to gather information that may be generalised to the whole population within statistically calculable margins of sampling error.
schedule	A media schedule provides details of proposed or booked advertising, stating the medium, stations, titles, space formats, dates and costs, etc.
seasonality	Dynamic whereby some brand sales are strongly related to the time of year.
share deal	A deal in which a media owner guarantees a specific price or service in return for a guaranteed sum of money.
share of voice	In the media context this applies to the advertiser's share of impressions or ratings achieved in a specific time period. Often used a part of competitive analysis.

sheetage	Term used to describe poster size in the UK.
site classification	A means of evaluating and grading poster sites from variables such as type of road, traffic volume, town or city, district proximity of the nearest sales outlet, lighting, obstruction from other objects, etc.
six sheet	Poster site commonly seen at bus stops and in shopping locations (1.8m x 1.2m).
solus	An advertisement that that has no commercial competition.
spill in	The degree to which advertising is seen outside the specific region intended.
split run	The ability to or the tactic of changing copy by region to elicit differing responses to advertising messages.
split transmission	The ability of a radio station to provide different services on its AM and FM frequencies.
sponsorship	The Official ITC definition states: "Where an event or a programme or any part of its cost of production or transmission are met by an organisation or persons other than a broadcaster or television producer, with a view to promoting its own or another's name or trademark, image, activities, products, or other direct or indirect interests."
spot colour	Two-colour press ad, often predominately monochrome.
spot rating	The estimated audience for a specific commercial slot, expressed as a percentage of the total target audience. Spot ratings are the units of currency for buying and selling television airtime.
storyboard	Drawings and words that visualise how a television advertisment will look.

strategic trawl	A semi-structured thought process to bring together relevant information on the brand.
strike rate	Daily, weekly or monthly patterns of advertising most commonly used for television laydowns.
subscription TV	Television channels requiring a subscription to view. The signals are scrambled to stop non-subscribers from viewing by means of a coded signal.
supersite	A poster panel whose size is 96 sheet (12m x 3m) or larger.

T

TGI — Target group index. Survey of consumers' usage and purchasing habits of a wide range of products and services which can be cross-tabulated with media consumption and attitudes. The survey is continuously conducted throughout the year, giving a total of 25,000 respondents aged 15+. The survey is published twice a year and is available on line to subscribers. TGI is used by advertisers and agencies to develop advertising and media strategies. There are additional specific surveys on 55+, youth and upmakret (AB) affluent consumers.

TSA — Total survey area. The transmission area of a radio station.

TVR — Television rating. One TVR is 1 per cent of any given audience.

tabloid — A newspaper format half the area of a broadsheet.

target consumer segement — A description of the relevant consumers that a brand is targeted at.

television laydown — Media plan that indicates detail of television airtime to be bought.

terrestrial television — Traditional delivery of the television signal that relies on land-based transmitters.

top and tail — When a television commercial is deliberately repeated at the beginning and the end of a commercial break for creative effect.

tracking studies — Continuous research that monitors a brand's performance in the marketplace.

traffic	Percentage of a publication's readers claiming to have read or looked at specific pages or elements of a publication.
traffic count	A count of the movement of people or vehicles past a given location, usually an outdoor site.
transponder	Device on a satellite which retransmits specific signals for television.
tube card	Posters seen on the inside of the London Underground.
twins	A poster package comprising two 48 sheets juxtaposed for creative effect.

U/V

U & A tracking surveys	Market research to understand usage and attitude towards a product or service.
USP	Unique selling proposition, i.e. something that is unique to your brand that you can communicate to potential consumers.
universe	The maximum potential audience meeting given criteria.
VAI	Visibility adjusted impacts. A method of measuring the number of people who view a poster site. VAIs use computer technology to measure eye movement when passing a site and are calculated by measuring this information against the gross number of people who pass the site. The better the panel, the closer the VAI to the gross number.
VFD	Verified free distribution. A monitoring system for free local newspapers.
vertical publication	Publications dealing with a specific topic and with narrow audience appeal.
video on demand	On demand instant access to television programmes.
voidage	Unsold poster capacity.
voucher	A discount offered to advertisers who reach a specified level of expenditure specified on a media owner's ratecard.
volume discount	A copy of a publication that acts as proof of an advertisement's appearance in a specific publication.

W/X/Y/Z

wear out When a campaign's effectiveness diminishes due to prolonged over-exposure of the advertisement.

web page A single HTML file when viewed on the world wide web to provide a document of information or entertainment.

website The body of information for a particular domain name. Typically made up of web pages.

weighting Factoring of statistical data or sample to be representative of the population. Can also refer to an area of specific consideration on which a higher than expected share of advertising resource is expended.

yield Average unit or revenue per unit of advertising space.

zapping Rapid channel switching or surfing via a remote control.

List of Helpful Addresses

1. **Advertising Standards Authority**
   2 Torrington Place
   London WC1E 7HW
   Tel: 0171 580 5555

2. **Association of Independent Radio Contractors**
   (Now - Commercial Radio Companies Association)
   77 Shaftesbury Avenue
   London
   W1V 7AD
   Tel: 0171 306 2603

3. **Audit Bureau of Circulation**
   Black Prince Yard
   207-209 High Street
   Berkhamstead
   Herts HP4 1AD
   Tel: 01442 870800

4. **Audits of Great Britain**
   Westgate
   London
   W5 1UA
   Tel: 0181 967 0007

5. **British Market Research Bureau**
   Hadley House
   79-81 Uxbridge Road
   London W5 5SU
   Tel: 0181 566 5000

List of Helpful Addresses

6. **Broadcasters Audience Research Bureau Ltd (BARB)**
   Glenthorne House
   Hammersmith Grove
   London W6 0ND
   Tel: 0181 741 9110

7. **Cable Communications Association**
   The 5th Floor
   Artillery House
   Artillery Row
   London SW1P 1RT
   Tel: 0171 222 2900

8. **CACI**
   CACI House
   Kensington Village
   Avonmore Road
   London W14 8TL
   Tel: 0171 602 6000

9. **Central Office of Information**
   Hercules Road
   London SE1
   Tel: 0171 928 2345

10. **Cinema Advertising Association (CAA)**
    12 Golden Square
    London W1R 3AF
    Tel: 0171 534 6363

11. **Incorporated Society of British Advertisers (ISBA)**
    44 Hertford Street
    London W1Y 8AE
    Tel: 0171 499 7502

12. **Institute of Practitioners in Advertising (IPA)**
    44 Belgrave Square
    London SW1X 8QS
    Tel: 0171 235 7020

13. **Joint Industry Committee for Regional Research (JICREG)**
    Bloomsbury House
    74-77 Great Russell Street
    London WC1B 3DA
    Tel: 0171 636 7014

14. **Office for National Statistics**
    (formerly the Central Statistics Office)
    1 Drummond Gate
    London SW1
    Tel: 0171 233 9233

15. **Outdoor Advertising Association**
    Summit House
    27 Sale Place
    London W2 1RY
    Tel: 0171 298 8035

16. **Periodical Publishers Association (PPA)**
    Queens House
    28 Kingsway
    London WC2B 6JR
    Tel: 0171 404 4166

17. **Radio Advertising Bureau**
    77 Shaftesbury Avenue
    London W1V 7AD
    Tel: 0171 306 2500

18. **Radio Joint Advertising Research (RAJAR)**
    Collier House
    163-169 Brompton Road
    London W1V 7AD
    Tel: 0171 584 3003

Index

A

agency/client relationship
   administration 127-8, 132
   briefing 125
   creative judgement 126-7
   creative process 131-2
   strategic thinking 130-31
   teamwork 128-9
   timing 124-5
   understanding your client's business 129-30
account management 87-8
administration 127-8, 132
advertising
   agencies *see* advertising agencies
   and attitudes 3-4, 35
   back to basics approach 16
   benefits of 8-10
   as communications tool 24, 83
   cost of campaigns 173-4
   coverage 169-70
   and desire 4
   effects on consumer behaviour 70-76
   evaluating effects 69
   flow of logic 19
   frequency 170-1
   as market planning 15-16
   noticeability of 83
   objectives of 2-8, 66, 68-9
   and perceptions 3-4, 35
   planning 162-3
   production process 51-62
   and reassurance 5
   representation of idea 43-4
   versatility of 1-2
   where 172-3
advertising agencies
   account management 87-8
   appointing 94-6
   appraisal 100-2
   assessing 96-7
   creative department 89-90
   media department 92-4
   planning department 89
   production department 90-92
   remuneration 102-6
   structure 31-2, 87
advertising/consumer interaction 76
advertising production process 51-62
agency brief *see also* briefing
   amalgam model 107, 109
   development 107-8
   perfecting 117-19
agency producer 56-7
airtime, cinema 152-3
amalgam model,
   agency briefs 107, 109
animatics 43
appraisal, of advertising agencies 100-2
area testing 74-5
art buyer 51, 91
art director 90
attitudes, and advertising 3-4, 35
Audience Guarantee Plan 152-3
Audit Bureau of Circulations (ABC) 148

auditing 106
Audits of Great Britain (AGB) 155
awareness 3, 77

B

BBC radio 160
behaviour measures 84
benefits
    analysis of 9
    definition 9-10
    emotional 11-12, 110
    generation of 40
    isolation 12
    rational 10, 109-10
blind/branded product test 81
brain 137-8
brand core 111
brand description 111
brand effects 76, 82
brand essence 108-10
brand marketing planning, and research 33-6
brand measures 84
brand model 65
brand name 111
brand personality 111
brand positioning 40-41, 66, 110-13
brand profile 77-79
brand review process 34-6
brand salience 76-7
brand situations 67-8
brand size 79
brand vision 119
brand/consumer relationship 79-80
brand/price relationship 81
brands
    benefits of 111
    developing 63
    emotional elements 110
    how they work 64-8
    marketing objectives 37
    rational elements 109-10
    sustaining 63, 64
brief *see* agency brief

briefing 119-22, 125
British Telecom (BY+T) 57
Broadcasters' Audience Research Board (BARB) 155
BSkyB 158-59
BT 57
budget restraints 31
burst campaign 170

C

client/agency relationship
    administration 127-8, 132
    briefing 125
    creative judgement 126-7
    creative process 131-2
    strategic thinking 130-31
    teamwork 128-9
    timing 124-5
    understanding your client's business 129-30
cable television 158-59
Carlton 153, 157
casting 57, 59
Central Office of Information (COI) 164
Central Statistical Office (CSO) 164
Channel 4 156-57
Channel 5 158
cinema advertising 43, 44, 147, 151-3, 173
colour separation 55
commercial strategy 114
commission 102-4
communication
    and advertising 7
    and strategic trawl 20-23
    objectives 37
    tools 23-30
communication mix statement 113-14
communications, integrated 30-32
company benefits 9
competitive advantage 11, 18
competitive set 112
competitive strategy 18

competitor advertising 73
computer modelling 93
consolidation 6
consumer/advertising interaction 76, 82-4
consumer/brand attachment 80
consumer/brand relationship 79-80
consumer insights 112
consumer involvement 144-6
consumer panels 36, 71, 72
consumer perceptions, of a brand 77-81
consumer response 83
consumer sophistication 31
consumer usage 72
consumers
  behaviour of 64, 72-3
  and brands 77-81
  research on 35
copywriters 90
corporate philosophy 32
Coutts, Derek 57
coverage 169-70
creating awareness 3
creating desire 4
creating sales 2-3
creative brief 114-17, 122-3
creative department, advertising agencies 89-90
creative development 41-2, 44
creative judgement 126-7
creative office 139
creative process 131-2, 140-42
creative services 51-2
creative work, judging 142-4
creativity, definition 137-8

D

demographics 112, 115, 164
demonstration 6
depth interviews 43
desire, and advertising 4
differential benefits 9
differentiation, of brands 111
digital television 161

direct effects on a brand 76
direct marketing 25
directors 55-6, 57-8
discipline 54
disposable nappies 5
distribution change 73
double benefits 9

E

econometric modelling 75-6
econometrics 75-6
effective frequency 170-2
emotional benefits, of advertising 11-12
emotional elements, of brands 110
emotional positionings 66
enquiry generation 6
executional elements 42
exhibitions 28-9

F

Fairy Liquid 12
fees 104
FHM 150
filming 59-60
final pre-production meeting 58-9
Financial Times 148, 149
flow of logic, and advertising 19
focus groups 42
focused marketing mix 18-19
48s (poster size) 154-5
four Ps 16-17
frequency, of advertising 169-70
functional positionings 66

G

Galaxy chocolate 13-14
global village 31
GMTV 156

H

Hartley, J R 14

I

ideas, defining 138-40
illustrators 52
Independent Radio 160
insight 12-14
integrated communications 30-32
internal agency creative brief 122-3
ITV 156-7

J

Joint Industry Committees 164
judging creative work 142-4

K

key frame boards 43, 44
Koestler, Arthur 139

L

Laser 157
left brain 137-8
Lipman, Maureen 57
Loaded 150
Lucozade 4

M

magazines 149-51, 173
major promotions 73
market definition 112
market structure, outdoor advertising 154-5
marketing
  concept 16-19
  definition 16
  objectives 69
media, choice of 165
media department 92-4
media fragmentation 31
media globalisation 31
media intelligence 93
media planner 92-3
media planning
  checklist 174-5
  medium selection 165-7
  preparation 162-3
  response to advertising 167-9
  strategy 163-5
media research 93, 164
merchandising 29-30
Morris, Jan 139

N

narrative tapes 43, 44
national newspapers 148-49
negotiation 102
Nescafé 57
Nestlé 57
non-television buying 92-3
noticeability, of advertising 83

O

objectives, of advertising 2-8, 66, 68-9
observation, of effects of advertising 74
outdoor advertising 43, 44, 153-5, 173

P

payment by results 2, 104-6
perceptions, and advertising 3-4, 35
performance related payments 105
photographers 52
photomatics 43
pitching 94-100
planning
  and advertising agencies 89
  media department 92-3
    see also media planning
  process of 16
portfolio positioning 17-18
positioning map 112
posters 43, 44, 153-5, 173
post-production process 61-2
power tools 6
pre-pre-production meetings 54
pre-production meetings 55-6, 58-9

presentation, traffic flowchart system 62
press
    ads 43, 44
    cost of campaigns 173
    flowchart 53
    national newspapers 148-9
    and print production 91
    share of total advertising 147
pre-testing
    brand effect 46-9
    brief assessment 49
    guidelines 49
    sales effect 45-6
price change 73
print and press production 91
print flowchart 53
producers 56-7, 59-60
production heads 91
productive indolence 139-40, 141
progress department 91
prompted awareness 77
protection of position 6
pschyographics 112, 115
public relations 27
purchasing 70

Q

qualitative research 36, 38-9
Quality of Readership Survey (QRS) 150-1
Quirke, Pauline 57

R

radio
    cost of advertising 173
    independent 160
    listenership 159-60
    share of total advertising 147
    stations 160
    and television production 91-2
Radio Joint Audience Research (RAJAR) 159
rates of commission 103-4
rational benefits, of advertising 10

rational elements, of a brand 109-10
readership, of magazines 150-1
reasons for buying 5
reassurance, and advertising 5
Reeves, Rosser 9
reinvention 67, 82
remuneration 102-6
research
    for brand marketing planning 33-6
    and brand positioning 40-41
    and creative brief 38-9
    for creative development 41-2
    processes 36
    qualitative 36
response 167-9
retail audit 71-2
right brain 137-8
roadside advertising 153
Robson, Linda 57

S

sales, creating 2-3
sales promotion 26-7
satellite television 158-9
scores, interpreting 48-9
scripts 59, 61
shoots 55
single-minded proposition 112, 115-16
6s (poster size) 154-5
Smith, Tony 57
socio-economic factors 35
soundtracks 43
sponsorship 28
standard benefits 9
strategic thinking 130-31
strategic trawl 19-23
Sun, The 148-9
Surf 57
sustainable competitive advantage 11

T

target consumers 18, 163
Target Group Index (TGI) 164-5
teamwork 128-9
technological developments 31
television
    advertising 43, 44
    cost of campaigns 173
    and radio production 91-2
    share of total advertising 147
    viewing 155-6
television buyer 93-4
television rating points 168-9
ten-point pitch guide 97-100
Thompson, Daly 4
Times, The 148, 149
tracking surveys 36, 82
traffic control 51
traffic flowchart system to client presentation 62
transport advertising 153
TSMS 157
typographers 91

U

U & A/tracking surveys 36, 82
unique selling proposition 9
uniqueness 144
unprompted awareness 77
usage 71

V

validation 46
Volkswagen 143-4

W

where to advertise 172-3
Willott Kingston Smith 105

Y

Yellow Pages 14, 145